SILENT OVERCOMER

SILENT OVERCOMER

Trauma comes in all shapes and sizes!

TRACEE L. HUNT

MHS, SPHR, SHRM-SCP

Foreword written by Best Selling Author,

Maysa Akbar, Ph.D., ABPP

ACADEMY
PRESS

For permission requests, write to the below address:

Tracee L. Hunt
921 Pleasant Valley Ave., Ste. 130
Mount Laurel, NJ 08054

The opinions expressed by the Author are not necessarily those held by PYP Academy Press.

Ordering Information: Quantity sales and special discounts are available on quantity purchases by corporations, associations, and others. For details, contact the author at www.traceelhunt.com.

Edited by: Malka Wickramatilake, Carol Jones, Nan Price
Cover design by: Aaniyah Ahmed
Typeset by: Medlar Publishing Solutions Pvt Ltd., India

Printed in the United States of America.

ISBN: 978-1-951591-59-5 (paperback)
ISBN: 978-1-951591-60-1 (ebook)

Library of Congress Control Number: 2021904754

First edition, March, 2021

The mission of the Publish Your Purpose Academy Press is to discover and publish authors who are striving to make a difference in the world. We give marginalized voices power and a stage to share their stories, speak their truth, and impact their communities. Do you have a book idea you would like us to consider publishing? Please visit PublishYourPurposePress.com for more information.

 PYP Academy Press
141 Weston Street, #155
Hartford, CT, 06141

Disclaimer

First and foremost, I must give thanks, honor, and praise to God from whom all blessings flow.

I dedicate this book to the love of my life and soul mate, my husband, Benjamin III (31 years and counting); my two amazing children, Benjamin IV and Taylor Lynn; and my awesome Fab 5: Michelle, Torrye, Sheila, Kelli, and Beth—the true order in which they came into my life. They all have loved me unconditionally and supported me in many ways through the various stages of my life. I must also thank Brownette, who has been a significant source of strength and encouragement that words cannot describe. Her unwavering and often quiet support has truly made a positive impact in my life's journey.

I must thank my mother for being the best mother she knew how to be and for leading me toward one of the most significant choices in my life that has allowed me to be who I am today. Please know that you are forgiven, and my only hope is that you can understand how important this book was in my healing process, and hopefully the healing of others. Daddy, you are forever appreciated for just being you. Barry, you were my first hero and Christopher, you were my first opportunity to learn how to truly love a little being!

TABLE OF CONTENTS

FOREWORD

Dr. Maysa Akbar, PhD

I have known Tracee for over five years. We met during a National Minority Supplier Development Council convention in New York City during the winter of 2015. We were both there for women-owned minority businesses that represented the sector of thriving entrepreneurs. My first encounter with Tracee was during a group discussion where we were tasked to tackle the "hard stuff" related to the entrepreneurial journey. As a clinical psychologist, I automatically study the room right off the bat. I am quick to identify who is shy or slow to warm, and those who are gregarious and come across as natural leaders. Tracee immediately caught my attention as being the latter. She had a commanding presence that was engaging and contagious. Her larger than life smile was infectious, and it was clear that she was the epidemy of confidence, through and through.

I saw the beautiful exterior that made her a magnetic leader during the work session. I saw what everyone else saw...and more. I saw beyond the armor, and it was not as shiny as her exterior presented. Deep in her eyes I saw the woman inside— the one who has been through hard things in life and had survived them. Tracee had mastered the capacity to show up in the world exactly the way she wanted people to see her, and how she likely wanted to see herself. On the outside she was dressed to the tee, with flawless makeup and shoulders back as she stood tall in her stilettos. She was the real deal, the full package. On the inside, I saw the insecurity, anxiety, and the little girl she kept hidden. I saw her profound emotional pain, I saw her history of abuse, and I saw her trauma. How? Because trauma knows trauma. We find each other.

That encounter was the beginning of a dynamic relationship with Tracee where I began to trust her enough to share the challenges I was experiencing in my business. I hired her Human Resources (HR) firm to consult with my behavioral health clinic, Integrated Wellness Group. She was brilliant— skilled far beyond expectation, not just in HR policy, procedure, and infrastructure, but also in business strategy and acumen. She was the missing puzzle piece to propel my business to the next level. As we got to know each other better, I told her about my journey to becoming a new author. I shared with her my fears and trepidations, and the challenges I faced in sharing my childhood story. She was one of the first readers of my book, *Urban Trauma: A Legacy of Racism.* She called me right after she read the book and I could hear the lump in her throat as she said, "I didn't know," and "me too."

Tracee is a spiritual woman who is a survivor. She has grown into feeling comfortable with who she is on the outside and with the little girl no one nurtured who lives inside. She's become gentler and patient with herself and has begun to love herself the way she should have always been loved: unconditionally. This book is not just about Tracee's life story, nor just about the insurmountable obstacles she has overcome, silently and in the shadows. No, this book represents a powerful movement of women from all walks of life relieving themselves from generational trauma. It is about recalibrating. Tracee demonstrates to her reader how she interrupted the vicious cycle of pain and abuse that was passed down in her family, and in many communities, more specifically in those of color. This book is about a new legacy built on hope, inspiring each and every one of us to seek our liberation, revel in our emotional freedom, and stand in our truth—because of our story, not in spite of it.

PREFACE

This book is written from a place of healing and forgiveness and is not in any way meant to villainize or focus on blame, but instead to convey a message of how to overcome versus being defeated. This book will give the reader permission to see herself/himself as an overcomer who "achieved in spite of" and be okay that her/his life does not align with the perfect story. The reader will be reaffirmed and/or come to the realization that trauma comes in all shapes and sizes, and that no one has the right to define or minimize what, who, or how she or he was traumatized. The reader will have the opportunity to reframe the trauma in her or his life to create a positive focus that is beneficial to the overall healing process. The ultimate goal is to encourage, uplift, and motivate the reader in a way that compels one to recognize that no matter the level of triumph or struggle, success will continually have to be created and redefined along life's journey.

The soul-bearing, no-holds-barred format of this book, from varying perspectives and walks of life, allows the reader to see herself or himself and to know that the ability to turn life's trauma into life's triumphs is indeed possible, even when it appears intangible. Reframing not only will support the healing process, but also provides the reader with the opportunity to assess her or his own life story and reframe those areas that will make a positive impact in her or his life today.

Reframing, which is also referred to as cognitive reframing and used by many therapists, is when a situation is looked at from a different perspective. The author looked at the negative situations and trauma in her life and made the choice to place a positive reframe on them. The positive perspective created the space for healing and forgiveness to take place. It is through this process that the author hopes the reader will also be able to look at her/ his own personal situations through a new lens. Successful authors, educators, business owners, and executives alike convey their oneness and association in experiencing trauma and overcoming tough circumstances through determination and fortitude that allows them to navigate the road to success, despite many obstacles along the way.

It is the author's hope that you are invigorated and challenged to face your trauma and reframe how it has shaped your life for the better, no matter your current circumstance or situation, whether amazing or not so amazing.

So please appreciate this journey of perpetual trauma and victory, and know that you too are, or can be, a silent overcomer.

CHAPTER ONE

TRAUMA IN UTERO

It's not about where we start,
but what we make of the journey.

L ike everyone, my journey began in the womb. Unlike everyone, the start of my journey was based on trauma and the struggle to survive. An embryo already has the fight of its life to sustain viability throughout the gestational period, which is the sole purpose for prenatal care. But being conceived under less than favorable circumstances and having the pregnancy deemed a total blunder, the struggle for existence became exponential. This was the beginning of my existence— an existence of being unwanted. While there was always the feeling of not being wanted, it did not become clear until years later. Imagine being trapped inside a space that despises your very existence. Then add the element of struggle to the equation and it is the recipe for the ultimate rejection. Here I was, the child born to a mother who in no way wanted to be pregnant because of the most humiliating circumstances. I was convinced that the very sight of me had to be traumatizing for her and I felt it. I was later told the stories of how the housing situation was not the best and how hard it was to make ends meet, which further confirmed my feelings. I can only speculate as to the level of anger and frustration my mother felt while carrying me; however, I can establish first-hand how it manifested in my life through how I was treated. Yet there was still so much more to the story I would not piece together until many years later.

Born into a volatile situation, I became the shadow of my brother, Barry, who was always there to watch over me. My clearest memories start around the age of five. I thought all five-year-old kids had seven-year-old brothers who played such a major role in their upbringing. My brother was my first real-life hero. He was required to watch over me and I'm sure it wore on him at times, whether he even realized it or not at such a young age. He looked out for me at home, when we were with the babysitter (dear old Ms. Hazelwood), outside playing, and on the five-block walk to school. This was normal life for me. He was the one who made me feel cared for up to this point. Unbeknown to me, I was already experiencing the natural human desire to be loved and accepted.

In addition to my brother, I had my grandparents. I am sure I spent a lot of time with them prior to the age of five, but my memories of them are from five years old and onward.

2

This is when everything became very vivid for me. My amazing grandmother, Lottie C., was five-foot, one-inch tall and all of 120 pounds soaking wet, with very dark brown skin. She was a homemaker who had jobs early on, but not during my lifetime. My dear grandfather, George T. Hawkins Sr., stood five-foot, six-inches tall, and maybe 145 pounds. He was so light skinned that he could pass for Caucasian. As a little girl, I questioned his race in my own mind, but it was not important enough for me to inquire. This did, however, frame my thinking relative to colorism later in life.

Grandma and Grandpa were the two people who I could trust most at my young age because they defined the only certainty in my brother's and my life. We would be at their house every Friday after school until Sunday evening, when we got picked up by my mother. We only saw our mother between Sunday evening and Friday morning, and that was really just to go through the motions of the weekly routine: go to school in the morning, get picked up from the babysitter, have dinner, and entertain each other until bedtime. I thought this was normal—didn't every child spend all their quality time with their grandparents? Little did I know that this very routine was birthing the power of suppression as a coping mechanism for the rejection and unwantedness that I was beginning to feel.

Nonetheless, my escape route and my ability to overcome were handed to me on a silver platter on a weekly basis. This is where and when Grandma became my saving grace. My brother was anointed the chosen one, which I later learned was status quo for the men in my family—they had always been favored

3

over the women—and I was merely his shadow. After spending Monday through Friday as a mere afterthought, Grandma's house allowed me the ability to shine, be adored, and loved on. After school on Friday, I would go to my grandparents' small shotgun house that sat on the corner of 16th and Yandes. It was a twin, but there were never any neighbors to live in the adjoining house because my grandfather had bought it. Talk about having a false sense of what well-to-do looked like. The houses were never refurbished to create a unified structure, but instead one remained dusty and creepy, and was used as a storage space and play area for my brother and me. It had a ping-pong table and was home to our bikes. The view from the east was a vacant lot, the view from the west was a car wash, and the view from the north was the pool hall where my grandmother would pull tickets. Further down the street from the vacant lot was the fish market and Jerry's corner store, also known as "Redfront." My grandparents' home was one of the best houses in a bad neighborhood and it was my weekly sanctuary.

On most days, we were welcomed with a snack Grandma knew both my brother and I would be happy to eat. The smells of homemade banana pudding, peach cobbler, or fried apples linger with me to this day. Canned peaches, on the other hand, I can do without. The peaches were fine, but that cloying syrup they came in turned me off to canned peaches to this day.

I always looked forward to the weekend, knowing it would be free of tension and scolding, one filled with laughter, lightheartedness, discovery, and the unexpected. In hindsight, my dearest Grandma was what one would call a functional alcoholic, and profane language was a part and parcel of her everyday vernacular. She smoked Pall Mall cigarettes with no filter (and oftentimes was mistaken for smoking marijuana), and her drink of choice was Fleischmann's gin, which she chased with water. She had unique tastes. She taught me how to play the dozens by having me shadow her on a regular basis. She would not hesitate to call someone a baldheaded "such and such," and her colorful personality and outspoken ways did get her the ire of many a neighbor. But my grandfather's standing in the community ensured that no one ever messed with my Grandma. She was a true matriarch of the neighborhood. The best part was that the very folks she was telling off, she was helping in the next breath. Go figure! Grandma's favorite dance was the Mississippi draw back, which she taught me at the ripe age of five—against my grandfather's better judgment, as the dance was somewhat sexy at that time.

On the complete other end of the spectrum was my grandfather, who we affectionately referred to as "Daddy." He did not drink or use profanity and was named "Man of the Year" on more than one occasion by different organizations in the city of Indianapolis, commemorating his life's work as a community contributor. He served as a coach for intramural sports for both girls and boys, including softball, volleyball, basketball, golf, and Golden Gloves boxing. He was a prominent figure at the local community center, serving as surrogate father and mentor to many. When my grandfather died at 80 years old, it was standing room only at his funeral, and his wake went on for what seemed like forever because so many people came from all walks of life, young and old. To this day, his picture appears on a billboard situated on the vacant lot where my grandparents' inviting house once stood. They balanced out each other and provided me with a sense of family, for what it was worth. This odd balance of character and love shared by them provided me with a bit of respite, sandwiched between each dreadful week that had passed and the one that lay ahead.

The highlight of the weekend in my early years was Daddy bringing us fast food as a treat on Friday nights. He would also let us in on his secret stash of "Orange Slices candy". They were his favorite sweet treat and would become one of my favorites too. He kept them in a special drawer in the dining room bureau and would invite us over to it to indulge in them.

We would wake on Saturday mornings and have breakfast—pancakes that were awesome to me, but not so much for my brother. Later, we would walk to the corner store and ultimately end up playing in the side yard, which was adjacent to the other houses' front yards. Grandma sat in her lawn chair and we made do with makeshift chairs made from milk crates. Grandma smoked her unfiltered Pall Malls and drank her cocktail. Even with all that she never missed having dinner on the table when my grandfather came home. They were special meals to me, even if they were simple. My favorites were navy beans and hot-water cornbread; hash, which was leftover roast beef made into a stew; and Indiana-style chili. I was coziest and felt safest when we would snuggle in with Grandma, even when that meant falling asleep together after watching scary movies like, *Sammy Terry*. I did not experience parental love from my mother, but my grandparents stepped into that gaping void without missing a beat.

Who could have ever thought that a functional alcoholic and a factory worker could bring so much joy and fulfillment to what can be characterized as a wounded and rejected five-year-old girl? But that's exactly what they gave me—the freedom to be myself, whatever that meant at such a callow age, without being an annoyance to the person who never wanted me. There are no real memories of good times with anyone outside of my grandmother and grandfather during this critically developmental time in my life.

Nonetheless, at a young age I had to make the choice to find the positive elements and build on them. Though I am certain the circumstances were not always perfect, it provided me a means of escape and the opportunity to overcome feeling unwanted, all while helping me to build what I did not know at the time was a positive self-esteem. It also did not hurt that I thought my name was "Pretty Tracee Lynn" up until about the age of five because it is what my Grandma told me. This spoke volumes for my grandmother's love for me because, in my own eyes, I was average at best. I would later learn that most children develop a healthy sense of self-esteem as early as age five, before even entering kindergarten. Thank goodness I was already well on my way to that because of my Grandma.

Little did I know that it was not the norm for little girls to only have their grandfathers as their father figure. Yet it was also the beginning of a life in which many statistical nuances would continue to manifest in various ways to shape my overall way of thinking, or not. It was not until I was able to pen this writing that I gained further insight into the treatment I had endured and the damage that it caused from a highly regarded child psychologist, who helped me see the things I would have to overcome later.

"Research suggests that as young as early childhood, children are able to depict when a system they are part of will support their success or keep them stagnant (Abram et al. 2004). This message of inadequacy that they receive is directly tied to how they engage with others, the support systems that they have, and the information that they internalize about themselves. When children encounter traumatic events, the effects can either build up their resiliency or lead to a lifetime of problems in multiple aspects of their lives, often disrupting their ability to self-actualize.

"The effects from traumatic events such as violence, abuse, loss, or abandonment are profound and long-lasting, some even to the extent of developing mental health concerns around alcoholism, depression, anxiety, paranoia, and other related disorders. Of course, trauma is a complex, yet a profoundly bendable life experience that happens to many children. Tracee turned her trauma and pain into power and purpose. Along with trauma, many stories of resilience are also birthed. By reframing, Tracee overcame her devastating start to life, beat all the odds, and manifested a loving and meaningful life to build a new legacy for her children of love, hope, and faith."

—Dr. Maysa Akbar, best-selling author, owner of Integrated Wellness Group, and a member of the Yale Child Study Team

As Dr. Akbar points out, even at a very young age, I was beginning to experience the traumas I would carry with me for decades. The messages I began receiving from those around me were already beginning to shape the messages I was giving myself. As an adult, it was important for me to reframe this time in my life by establishing how grateful I am that my mother did not abort me. For this period in my life, reframing required me to reflect on being grateful that I was born at all. I had to appreciate my mother for not getting an abortion, which she could have chosen to do. I reframed the negative feelings of being unwanted into the positive perspective of thankfulness for life. Remember that the process of reframing is simply to change your perspective on a given situation to give it a positive or beneficial meaning.

REFERENCE

Abram, K. M., Teplin, L. A., Charles, D. R., Longworth, S. L., McClelland, G. M., & Dulcan, M. K. (2004). Posttraumatic stress disorder and trauma in youth in juvenile detention. *Archives of general psychiatry*, *61*(4), 403–410.

I invite you to take a moment to reflect on any trauma you experienced at a very young age. Oftentimes, hearing another person's experiences of trauma can trigger our own stories. Contemplate the things that happened in your life as a young child and, if you are able, feel free to work openly on reframing those traumas.

What are you holding onto as it relates to your youngest childhood memories (up to age five) that you need to reframe? Be careful not to attempt to consolidate too much so that you will have a more positive reframe.

Challenging memories of my childhood up to age five are:

_____

_____

_____

_____

I make the choice to reframe those memories by restating them in the following way:

_____

_____

_____

_____

CHAPTER TWO

FROM ONE HOUSE TO THE NEXT, THE TRAUMA FOLLOWED

*Our very existence confirms that a bright spot
can be found in any situation—we have to
find the bright spot and reflect on it as often
as is necessary to get through.*

I began the next phase of my life, elementary school, attempting to identify where I fit in. I slept at my mother's house, which never felt like home at this stage of my life, Monday through Thursday. It was an apartment that consisted of two bedrooms, one of which was occupied by my mother and the other by my uncle, leaving Barry and me to share a sofa bed. My mother did her best to ensure that I was dressed nicely and that my hair was combed neatly so that in no way did I hinder the well put together image that was intended as a reflection of her. This was the same mother who was very quick

11

to tell me that I was not cute and to make harsh remarks about my eyes, which happened to be very big and still are. Comments like, "get out of my face with your bug-eyed self," were the norm. She would get so close to my face that I could feel her breath on my skin and her eyes piercing sharply into mine. It was the commentary that went along with any scolding, no matter the deed. Hence, I looked great on the outside, but was continually being broken down on the inside.

Both Barry and I (eight and six years old, respectively) headed to school each day, with Barry always astute at handling his normal duty of looking after me. This consisted of about a five-block, hand-holding walk to school #45, where Mrs. Franklin was my first grade teacher. Once in school, I was no longer under the command and control of my mother, who I was being taught to fear. Little did I know, I would begin treating my peers in the same manner as my mother treated me. This was evidenced when I got my report card and all my grades were good except for the one pertaining to "Social Habits," which was challenged on more than one occasion from second to sixth grade. The comments made by my teachers always pertained to my inability to connect appropriately with my peers. I wonder why? Could it have been that at this point I was continually yelled at, spoken down to, told that I would never be anything, getting a beating for any little thing? By my mother, of all people. So, little elementary me went to school and attempted to control that which appeared to be controllable for someone my size.

It wasn't as if I was trying to test the limits of how far this behavior would get me, but what I learned was that it would consistently get me as far as being "on punishment," for weeks at a time, sometimes for over a month, though I was still under the age of nine. Talk about exorbitant. It was probably a good thing that I did not know what exorbitant meant when I was young because I may have gotten punished or beaten for mentioning it. All punishments and beatings were extreme. I was no angel, but how much can a child between the ages of seven and nine do to be punished so severely?

Most of my memories of abuse and unwantedness can be traced back to very specific living situations. We moved a great deal when I was a child, living in five different places by the time I was 13 years old. This included moving back in with my grandparents, the one place where I truly felt loved. But two of those addresses epitomized some of the most significant trauma of my childhood.

When we lived at 22nd and Talbot, I recall getting a massive beating for not eating my vegetables and putting them behind the stove. I remember getting the beating and then being told that I could not have dessert for a week. Thank God for my grandmother; when Friday rolled around, I got to her house and a snack awaited me! She thought the beating was enough—I was only five years old at the time. There was no need to deprive me of dessert as well. There was also a time on Talbot

13

when the saying, "it takes a village," was really referring to me, as other family members beat me as well. I once received a beating for lying about who left splashed Kool-Aid in the sink. It was a summer afternoon, and Barry and I were outside playing with our neighborhood friends, but I had not cleaned up some splashed Kool-Aid in the sink before playing. I was certain to get a beating, so I took the chance on getting away with a lie. My uncle, who was also someone I adored, was allowed to beat me for the Kool-Aid incident in lieu of my mother, who was not home at the time. The beating was brutal, as his belt and the force behind it made it feel like an eternity. It was as though with each lash a part of me was being stripped away and nobody cared. It produced one of those cries where I was sniffling well beyond the actual tears, and all I was left to wonder was why I got beatings from any and everybody, and my brother did not get any—so I thought. I don't even recall him getting yelled at during my young years. Each strike I received left welts and scars, ensuring their effect lasted long after the initial beating.

I can replay it in my head so clearly, again and again, being called pop-eyed and bug-eyed, even though it was a known fact that I was very sensitive about how big my eyes were—they appeared even larger when I was a young child. My mother seemed to take particular pleasure when she resorted to her infamous kill Tracee's spirit comment: I was told to get out of her face with my ugly self. There was simply no refuge until the weekend. My brother could not help me and my mother's boyfriend—soon to become my stepfather—had little to nothing to say, as he was kept in his place by my mother and deliberately marginalized in his capacity to parent Barry or me, even once they were married. So, I was trapped with this mother who clearly despised me. When I woke on Saturday mornings, I found greater comfort and peace in the stale smell of my grandmother's gin over the sweet, perfumed smell of my mother. I identified the perfume merely as a cover-up for the venom that she so readily spewed.

The time spent at the house on 12th Street was a short, but especially traumatic time for me. This was when my mother and now stepfather, newly married, decided to buy a house. I was nine years old. The house was in what was then a nice neighborhood and was located directly across the street from Crispus Attucks High School, within blocks of my step-grandmother, and only a few blocks from the historic Madame C.J. Walker Building, where we were able to walk to the movie theater located inside. It was evident that the goal was to take the family to the next level; however, the same treatment for me followed us right into the house at the new address. To add another layer of complexity, my stepbrother moved with us. While he had visited off and on up until this time, now it was more permanent. And, of course, my mother had to spread what seemed to me to be her sparse attention and affection to yet another child, when most of it went to my brother in the first place. The mean treatment only intensified, as I did not fully understand that our time at this house would be short-lived before my mom and stepdad separated. I can recall one beating where my parents had company and we were doing something we were not supposed to be doing. The details of the atrocity remain fuzzy, but I distinctly remember being the only one who got a beating. Instead of waiting to render the lashing after the company left, I was held upside down by both feet and beaten without being allowed to cry, for it was not polite to cry when company was in the vicinity, as that may have caused embarrassment. Talk about torture. The most scathing thing about this story was, when discussed later, my mother thought it was funny. Even worse, it was justified for many years. This left such a feeling of worthlessness, though I would always laugh it off to keep the peace.

There was a void that even a weekend to Grandma's house could not fill. This could be characterized as textbook treatment that leads to a child's low self-esteem. This was the treatment that further taught me to fear my mother for my own safety. This was also a time when the extreme psychological abuse was like a runaway train. It was commonplace to be cursed at and slapped in the face. I was continually being told to shut up, so there was no getting my side heard, especially given the fact that I would already be deemed guilty. I learned to lie to get out of a situation as I wanted to get out of a beating and a tongue slashing at all costs. It was ironic how I was scorned for lying because of how much my mother "detested" liars, yet my entire life up to this point was really based on a lie.

The trauma was only magnified by the feeling that my step-grandmother did not accept my mother. It felt as if her perceived distaste for my mother was passed down to me as well, leaving me to ultimately feel that I too was not good enough. I remember there was a boy down the street named Booker (everybody called him Booger) who liked me. There is really no story to tell about Booker and me, as we were only nine years olds, but his showing me that he liked me was enough to keep the glimmer of self-esteem alive, the small glimmer that until then had only been lit by my Grandma. During our time on 12th Street, we did not go to our grandparents' house every weekend because we now had our stepbrother living with us. Whether that is the reason or not, it was my small child mind's understanding of why I did not get to see the one person who uplifted my self-esteem.

Barry was my consummate protector. Nonetheless, he could not protect me from the insane punishments of my mother. One of my punishments, which were always extreme and satisfied my mother's agenda in some way (I guess), affected my sacred time at my grandparents' and my church life. I had received a less than acceptable grade in social habits, which I am not excusing at all, but the punishment for the grade was to remain in the house for

17

six weeks without playing with my friends. And to top it off, it was Easter. This was a time in our culture and family history when all the kids went to church with their new Easter clothes and paraded around, feeling good about themselves. For me, this particular Easter was yet another time for my mother to strip away an additional layer of my self-esteem by ensuring my brother was amazingly handsome—as he always was—and making me stay home with Grandma, which under any other circumstances would be okay. My mother could have made me stay at the house on 12th Street instead of at my grandparents' house. But no, I was left to wait at Grandma's house until my brother and all my cousins came in after church with their new clothes and Easter candy, and then I had to explain to them what I had done that precluded me from joining in their Easter joy. Of course, my mother was nowhere around to witness the damage and humiliation she intentionally wanted to cause. Her mission was accomplished. Nonetheless, if I had not gotten the bad grade I could have participated, though I believe she would have found another reason to humiliate me in front of my extended family.

I also recall being summoned to the kitchen to be reprimanded for something. Whether big or small, it was always a monumental tongue lashing. In this case, she was cooking and while she was verbally disciplining me, she kept threatening to pour boiling water on me from a pot that she kept waving dangerously close to me. As I tried to back away in absolute terror, I was finally released with the parting words of, "get out of my face with your ugly self." So, I took my nine-year-old self, working to continually convince myself that I was Grandma's "pretty Tracee Lynn," back to my room and pondered on the thoughts of getting away from my mother forever. Though my young self could not comprehend it at the time, this was severe emotional abuse. So much abuse, trauma, and bad memories were attached to this address in such a short period of time that it could be characterized in my little mind as the house of horrors.

Even with all the moving, we still got to spend time with my grandparents. They took us to the amusement park, the state fair, and all the normal kinds of places kids usually went to with their parents. Even more monumental than the quality time spent with our grandparents was that my grandfather (Daddy) was the sole source of introducing me and my brother to a life in church. No matter where we lived, my mother—who never went to church during my time as a child, at least not until I left home at 19—would ensure that we were with our grandparents or dropped off at church for Sunday school from where our grandfather would either bring us home or we would be instructed to walk the one block to our grandparents' house. This gave Barry the opportunity to be responsible for me yet again.

The damage caused by the psychological trauma inflicted on a child can never be underestimated.

Now, being a mother myself, I understand that my mother had the control to establish the punishment. And for my mother, it was always about control. I can recall that at this point in my life—around nine years old—I was introduced to my mother's most damaging and repeated statement, that even today I cannot understand the need to say to a child. It was continuously drilled into my spirit as she would look me in the eyes and say: "I hold the key." She was conveying, in the most demeaning and penetrating way possible, that she totally controlled everything about me and that I should never forget it. Being parented by fear and intimidation was normal. It was a level of trauma that many say is equivalent to forms of physical abuse, of which I had my fair share. Nonetheless, it was the main ingredient of my source of resentment that would prove to be one of the motivating factors for me to succeed in life.

Studies have shown that enlisting a feeling of fear and intimidation in a child is defined as psychological abuse and is just as harmful as physical abuse. This abuse has consequences according to the 2018 Global Report on Children. Those consequences place children at a higher risk of perpetuating or being a victim of violence, depression, obesity, higher-risk sexual behaviors, and unintended pregnancies, as well as engage in the harmful use of tobacco, drugs, and alcohol. This would define one stage of my life.

When I was still nine years old, we moved in with my grandparents. Their neighborhood was very colorful, to say the least. Being one of the best houses in, what I did not know then, a rough neighborhood gave me a huge sense of security. Just picture the neighborhood, which is now the product of gentrification with a billboard of my amazing grandfather in the very spot where I once played. My feisty grandmother had a description of everyone on her block with a twist of humor that would always make her updates on the neighbors more fun once I moved away. The neighbor across the street was Ms. Overweight Peeping Tom, the neighbors next door were Mr. and Mrs. Prim and Proper, and then there was Mr. Bootleg Liquor Man, whose wife always served as the always-on-duty security guard. Next door to the liquor house was The Cat Lady, who seemed to have a million cats. Next door to her was The Dog House with way too many dogs and no leashes. The instructions from Grandma that mattered most were to walk past the dogs and make sure you do not let them smell your fear and, if you had to, just look them in the eyes. Then there were a few vacant lots before I came to the house of my three best friends—Kity Kat, Pete, and Skeet: a sister and two brothers. Go figure, but they were the best friends ever and we spent many days playing up and down my grandparents' street. Games like kickball and dodgeball and, not to mention, putting empty cans on my shoes to wear like high heels. Next was my brother's best friend's house. We were a constant fixture on the block as we all hung out together and had pure unadulterated fun. Maybe I was the only one oblivious to the fact that we were poor and we all existed in some form of dysfunction that was not clear to me at the time.

Nonetheless, this was a time of rebuilding and learning the power of choice. My mother, brother, and I moved back in with my grandparents. While, it may not have been the best for my mother—an adult moving back with her parents is never particularly healthy—it was awesome for me to be under the love and care of my grandmother on a regular basis. I did not realize how broken I was until I had the opportunity to be around Grandma every day again. Of course, sometimes her drinking got on my nerves, especially when I would peek and see the gin bottles hidden under the sofa cushions, but there was never a time that I would substitute it for the physical and mental abuse I sustained from my mother. It was during this stint with my grandmother, between the latter part of age nine to age 11, that I was reinforced and tested simultaneously. This was a time when my mother worked and had a social life, while I had plenty of time with my grandmother. Living in a nice house in a bad neighborhood created a unique juxtaposition—I was receiving all the nurturing and self-assurance that I was in desperate need of from my Grandma, but in a geographic area that would be described, even during that time, as indigent on many levels. Some of my fondest memories might be classified as dysfunctional to many.

The daily routine, especially in the summer, consisted of going to Redfront (also known as Jerry's) corner store. The walk was short and invigorating, as I was very comfortable and familiar with my surroundings. Grandma's house was on the corner, so I would cross the street to begin my journey. Across busy 16th Street I could see the pool hall where they ran numbers. This was an illegal version of the lottery that at the time did not exist—at least not in Indianapolis. I would then pass a few houses that faced the busy street before I came to Joe's fish market. My mouth watered and my nose sucked in the enticing smells of fried fish and French fries. I'd always hope that Joe's fried fish and fries would be on the potential dinner menu at Grandma's. My assignment was to get Grandma's cigarettes and I was given 50 cents of my own with which I faithfully bought five packages of Now and Later Candies and a Faygo pop. There must have been great fluoride in the water as I never had a cavity until I was an adult living in New Jersey. I also was saved by genetics because all the pop and candy we ate could have been dangerous. I would also walk to Frankovitz grocery, which entailed cutting through several neighborhoods consisting of abandoned houses, vacant lots and a slew of stray dogs—always remembering we were taught to look them in the eyes, so they did not detect our fear.

Frankovitz's was the grocery that had more variety than Jerry's corner store. The joy of going to Frankovitz's was having a larger candy selection; however, the dreaded part of the trip was when I had to wait at the entrance of the liquor store across the street and not move while Grandma went in to get her coveted bottle of Fleischmann's. While there were several questionable characters going in and out of the liquor store, I never felt afraid as I had such a feeling of security whenever I was with my grandmother. This was merely part of the process that I had to go through to have more time to bond with my best friend, Grandma. We would walk, talk, and laugh through the entire journey. She even taught me how to scratch my back on the light poles if nobody was around to take care of my itch. What I later realized is, she was teaching me amazing lessons about how to navigate my way through life, even with little support. We also spent lots of time in the yard, from which the largest dose of self-esteem was derived. This was another opportunity for Grandma to make me feel special. She named every flower that grew and seed she planted in her yard Pretty Tracee Lynn. Those moments were so powerful in a lifelong journey of overcoming.

There were traumas I experienced as a child that were not at the hands of my mother and happened while living with my grandparents. I had two of the most horrifying experiences on two occasions at Ms. Rose's house. Ms. Rose lived catty-corner from my grandmother and next door to Ms. Haliburton, who had what seemed like a hundred kids. Her house always smelled like food, and I associated it with her obesity—she was always cooking, eating, and drinking. I had to go to the bathroom, which happened to be next to a bedroom along the same hallway. The bedroom door was open and, lo and behold, there was Ms. Tiny (don't recall the relation to Ms. Rose) and a big fat man in the bed, naked. He looked like a huge, fat, wet walrus. I was absolutely traumatized to the point that I no longer had to go to the bathroom. I went back and told my grandmother and, of course, she cursed out everybody in the house and then we went home. The picture was permanently imprinted on my brain. I think it also sobered up Grandma and she went on to explain that they were all nasty and to just never leave her side if we were over there again. I accepted that and we never mentioned it again. Fast forward—it had to be in the same summer—that I was on my way back from the corner store and was cutting across Ms. Rose's backyard to go to Ms. Haliburton's house to hang out with her daughter who was close to my age. We were around 10 years old. As I was coming across the yard, which housed junk, matted grass, and dirt, Ms. Rose's brother, Steve (another obese person), summoned me to come over to him. I yelled and asked for what. He asked for me to just come to him for a second. I walked toward him, but did not get too close, yet I was close enough to hear him proposition me to perform a sexual act on him for money. Here I was with another situation at Ms. Rose's house. After the way my grandmother lit into them the first time, I was afraid to tell her about this. I also was afraid I was going to get in trouble for even giving him the chance to say anything to me. So, I took off running and went straight to my grandmother's and never even stopped at Ms. Haliburton's. I just ran to safety. Not fully understanding it at the time, this disgusting proposition could have caused an imprint on my psyche as it relates to my self-worth. Again, I made the choice not to make it my fault, but his. Remember, my savior Grandma had told me they were all nasty. Now I really believed her.

The next summer I was hired by my grand-aunt (my grandmother's sister), who was an amputee as a result of diabetes, to help with daily chores around her apartment. This was meant to be an opportunity to learn responsibility and to make money—it is still hard to believe that my mother allowed me to take the city bus at 11 years old to an even worse part of town and then walk five blocks to my aunt's house in the projects. I loved my little job, though I was subjected to being in the house with her son and his girlfriend on a regular basis. It would have been fine if I didn't have to hear them having relations behind their closed bedroom door. It was like hearing a live porn movie.

My walk to her house was scary. One day as I was walking down the street, a man was masturbating in his car. Listening to all the porn in the world would not

26

have prepared me for this. The meaning of sprint came to life when I had to take off running for fear that he was going to start the car and follow me. It was too much for an 11-year-old to take. I ran to my aunt's house and told her all about it. You would think my mother would have told me to stop going, but no, I was back on the bus the next day. I know I truly had a guardian angel. Someone once told me that the Lord takes care of babies and fools. I would like to believe that even though I was being held accountable like an adult, I was still more of a baby than a fool. The sad truth is that apart from small snippets, I have very little recollection of where my mother was in the middle of all that I was seeing and experiencing. I remember her going to work and then leaving the house most evenings to spend time with her friends. Grandma continued to be my rock and stability.

All the inner turmoil was manifesting in various ways at school. I was considered the girl who thought she was cute. My mother did always make sure that I was dressed nice as she felt it was a reflection of her, so there were a few girls who routinely treated me badly. In response to being treated horribly, I felt the need to prove that I was just as tough as they were—especially since I already had my fair share of being treated horribly by my own mother. The intersection of being emotionally neglected by my mother and the treatment by the mean girls at school highlighted just how wounded, angry, and hurt I was. I responded to what I was experiencing the

27

only way that felt normal to me, by treating those I felt I could control in a demeaning way. In my sixth grade class, there was a boy that was quite frail and I realized that I could beat him up. So, I did on at least three occasions. When we transitioned into seventh grade, he took karate. This was good for him and me, I guess, since it meant he could stand up for himself. I also remember beating up my own friend on the playground because she kept getting smart with me. I tore her shirt off and she had to run home shirtless and humiliated. I immediately felt horrible. This was a defining moment for me. I realized I needed to turn over a new leaf and stay clear of the "rock-em, sock-em" reputation and establish myself as a lady. The decision was just that quick. When I look back, I also think it was partially as a result of coming into my own. While I had not connected the fact that hurt people hurt other people, I knew that this was not who I wanted to be. I maintained this new leaf, though the treatment I received did not necessarily change. It also helped with my new image and appreciation for fashion, as I no longer had any desire to mess up my outfits by fighting and getting dirty.

Another dimension of my young self who was stacked with mixed emotions at any given time was my sense of compassion, which was much like that of my grandmother's as it pertained to me. I recall being placed in the seat next to the one girl in the class known for smelling like a two-day-old soiled Pamper. I was told by my teacher, Mr. Upson—who paddled me every day for chewing gum, though he was deemed legally blind because he only had peripheral vision and basically no direct vision—that he knew I would not be mean to her, but instead become her friend. Oddly enough, I did. Mr. Upson was also the teacher who encouraged me the greatest during my elementary years. There it was early on, my capacity to see past my own issues and trauma and support someone else. Yet, look at the dysfunction in this: I was respectful of the very person who paddled me every day but, of course, I was used to getting worse beatings at home. Little did I know this was another manifestation of daddy issues, not at all related to my grandfather.

Through it all, my grandparents were still able to instill in me some sense of security. Our grandfather introduced us to our haven during the school year. The local community center became our hangout after school. It was also where my grandfather worked part-time, in addition to his full-time job. He coached every sport one could imagine. My brother and I were introduced to everything from basketball, softball, and baseball to track and football. We learned to play pool, table tennis (ping-pong), and all the other table games available. The added bonus was that I got to hang out with my grandmother, work on puzzles, play cards, and watch soap operas, which my grandfather hated, and Elvis Presley movies! It was just fun being with and around them.

29

The final summer living with Grandma, before my mother was able to get an apartment for us, was one I will never forget. Barry was allowed to spend the summer with "his" father and I was left to be with my mother and grandmother. I was between 11 and 12 years old at this time, and as much as I loved my grandmother, I was at a stage in my life where I was more interested in hanging out. Unfortunately, I ended up spending an inordinate amount of time with my mother and a friend of hers, which only led to more traumatic experiences and trauma. It was a summer that I never wanted to remember.

I was experiencing things that I did not know how to categorize or process. I had a mother who lived in the same house but was mostly absent. She provided basic needs yet was extremely dogmatic and demeaning. I had a grandmother who was available all the time, full of love, but the relationship was evolving as I grew into a pre-teen. And to top it all off, the grandfather who I so adored in my early years was not as interesting for a girl in puberty who did not want to hang out at the rec center with him while he worked. Barry was working at the corner grocery store and was not around much either. At this point, little did I know how critical the male parent is in a young girl's life. I just knew something was missing and I had no one to turn to. It was a lot to process, making my ability to reframe my years from the latter part of age nine though age 12 extremely difficult. The traumas were numerous and ongoing.

How do you heal a wound that is still bleeding? More important, how do you heal a wound that no one acknowledges is a wound, except you?

I learned the importance of understanding that there are many stories like mine across various stages of life. As I experienced many successful people along life's journey who had similar stories, it is important to share their perspective on my experience as it relates to their individual journey.

"I felt invisible when my black father left my mother, two brothers, and myself for another woman—a white woman—and her children who lived around the corner from my home. These children attended the same schools and after-school activities as my brothers and me. These other children started to taunt me on the playground, referring to my father as their "daddy." While present in my life, my father was the primary source of emotional abuse and episodic involvement. I felt like I was never enough and was only good enough to be yelled at or discarded. To me, the white family had all the fun, and my black family was only useful to vent out anger and disappointment. I tried to make myself invisible when my father came around, so he would not see me and make disparaging comments that were hurtful. The fear of being the target of my father's venom and disappointment led to low self-esteem and a constant struggle to see myself as worthy or more than enough. The trauma of being left by my father for another family made me feel inadequate, unworthy, and led to dysfunctional relationships with men and trust issues later in life, which manifested itself as low self-esteem as a black woman."

—Dr. Stacy Holland, Principal of The Holland Group

Dr. Holland used her own experience of feeling invisible as a motivation to become an advocate for young people who live in communities with high rates of poverty and trauma to discover their talent and build their self-esteem. Her work has empowered young people to know their worth and learn how to overcome various challenges, and to build networks of caring adults who see and honor their potential.

The reframe for me during this period was very challenging. As a mom, I cannot fathom treating a child I birthed this way. However, I had to come to realize that hurt people, hurt people. My mother had to have been hurting and I was the one on whom she took out that hurt because I was the only one who she had enough control over to do so. I had to come to grips with the fact that I did not know (though I have drawn my own conclusion) and may never truly understand what motivated her to treat me as she did, but that I had to forgive her. I reframed this period as being a time when I learned how to navigate life in uncomfortable situations, and that there was at least a place where I could turn, even if it was only the gratifying foundational memories established by my grandmother. I developed a sense of knowing that if I got good grades and could be seen in a positive light at school, it could be beneficial to my cause.

I once again invite you to take a moment to reflect on any trauma you experienced in your elementary through junior high school years. It is important to keep in mind that hearing another person's experiences of trauma can trigger our own stories. Contemplate the things that happened in your life during your elementary school to junior high years and, if you are able, I encourage you to work openly on reframing those traumas.

What are you holding on to as it relates to your next level of childhood memories (age six—12) that you need to reframe? Be careful not to attempt to consolidate too much so you will have a more positive reframe.

Challenging memories of my childhood age six—12:

_____

_____

_____

_____

I make the choice to reframe those memories by restating them in the following way:

_____

_____

_____

_____

I may need to contact the following people to give them an opportunity to understand how I am working through my reframe process:

_____

_____

_____

_____

CHAPTER THREE

TRAUMA...DRAMA... AND JUST BEING A TEENAGER

*Every situation and circumstance contain
lessons that can prove to be beneficial
along life's journey.*

I embarked upon my teens when my brother, my mother, and I were living in an apartment. We remained enrolled in the school across the street from my grandmother's house, so that Grandma would have easy access if there was a need to go to the school, especially given my less than stellar record up through sixth grade. I recall having to catch the city bus everyday with my brother. While it was a time of bonding, it was also a time of truly understanding that he really was my faithful caretaker. As always, he was required to protect me, yet he never made me feel like I was a burden. Well, I may have been a burden that one time when I made us miss the bus because I stopped dead in my tracks when I saw two dogs mating and they had gotten stuck together. This is another image that forever will be engrained in my mind. To date, living the city life had not exposed me to such trivial moments as dogs mating, and I was transfixed. As protective as he was, however, he could not protect me from the ongoing psychological abuse my mother inflicted on me every time I was scolded. I was constantly told how ugly I was and that I was not going to be anything. It was so ingrained that all I wanted to do was to prove her wrong. Having children of my own made me recognize how damaging this was and how one can control the anger that spurs a parent to be mentally or physically abusive to a child.

I was in the seventh grade, living life in the only way I had known it—being blamed for most things and not getting much affirmation, unless it came from my grandmother, but still coping. I had successfully secured my initial place in the world of work, which would be considered exploitation of child labor today. I was working at the same corner store with my brother. He worked in the meat department and I worked stamping prices on groceries and stocking shelves. Life was good! I got paid in cash and did not have to ask my mother for as much money as before. I loathed having to ask for anything from the person I had been taught to fear. I loved my little job for two reasons: (1) I loved using the pricing stamper on all the canned goods and (2) it gave me another reason to stick around my grandmother's neighborhood after school.

Little did I know that my world was about to change on one hand and be turned upside down on the other. My mother, who was separated from my stepfather, informed my brother and me that she was pregnant. I was 12 and my brother was 14. I had reached puberty by that time, and all I could think of, but not say, was, "you just started telling me not to get pregnant and here you are pregnant." In my young mind I had not processed that she was still married even though she was separated, but instead all I could see was that they were not together. And, now I was going to fall even lower on the totem pole.

Here is where things got turned upside down, and it all started as a result of a mere conversation where it was conveyed to me that my brother—who I esteemed highly—was only my half-brother. I was devastated, as I believed that if you have the same mother then you are whole brother and sister. How wrong I was. My world came crashing down like a ton of bricks. The one person, other than my grandparents, whose bond I cherished more than life itself, was not my whole brother but my "half-brother."

This was the one thing that challenged me to go to the person who I was terrified of pissing off: my mother. Notwithstanding the fact that she might be on the attack when I approached her on such a sensitive subject, I did not care and was willing to upset the apple cart. So, I put on my big girl panties and headed straight for my mother. By the time I approached her, fear gripped me, yet I asked her if my brother and I were half brother and sister. In that moment, I might have been more at ease asking to wear booty shorts to church. This question required her to be open about my paternity. Mind you, it had never burdened my mother to discuss my paternity with me, and I was almost high school age. Talk about not knowing what you do not know. As I approached the cusp of 13, my mother told me that the man I had been introduced to on a few occasions as my brother's father was also my father. All these years, I had been made to believe that my father—or the idea of who my father was—had abandoned me as a young baby. My emotions were so mixed. On one hand, I was extremely excited that my cherished brother and I were, in fact, whole siblings. On the other hand, I went into a mode of just processing. I felt cheated, lied to, wronged, looked over, undervalued, and just not important enough to be told the truth. Beyond all else, I had been living part of a lie. But God forbid I would have the chance to express how I felt because, as usual, it was always about my mother's struggle as part of the normal routine of deferring and deflecting. I had been okay all this time having a stepfather who was nice, but not very involved in my upbringing, but this was ridiculous and overwhelming. In my 12, almost 13-year-old mind, I just could not fathom how a mother would allow her child to believe that the child's father had abandoned her, all so the mother could save face for how and with whom the child was conceived. I immediately began to go over and over in my mind, asking who else knew this and did not tell me. At this point, I did not know which was worse, not knowing who my father was at all, or finding out that my father had been kept from me to save my mother's reputation.

At first chance I asked my grandmother, and she said she had a feeling that this was the case all these years. But who is to say that she had been sworn to secrecy? However, I did learn that my grandfather despised my brother's father—this is how I still referred to him at this point—because he was older than my mother and was known to be a "ladies' man." This could have been the reason my mother did not want to acknowledge to the world that she fell for his charm twice. Nonetheless, a hefty price to make a child pay to save face.

I had a million questions and wanted the opportunity to meet with the man who I thought, for all these years, was not my father. I learned later that besides also fathering my brother, he had fathered many others. My biological father came to our house, picked me up, and took me out for the first time when I was 12 years old. He took me shopping to buy anything that I wanted. Even with my wish being granted, my first question to him was, "why didn't you tell me?" He told me that it was largely my mother's choice to keep him a secret. I imagine he had nothing to lose because he apparently had no shame in what he stood for. He was kind, funny, and very good looking. My brother looks just like him. I guess there was no room to complain about the gene pool that he provided. As the after-noon wore on, he asked me what I wanted. All I could think of was how much I wanted some amazing jeans that I had seen. At $59, they were very expensive—the True Religion jeans of the '80s. When he bought them for me it completely infuri-ated my mother. She cursed at the top of her lungs—which was not unusual—that he had done nothing all these years and now he walked right in and bought a pair of jeans so he could have my admiration. While I was just happy to get the jeans—we did not get a lot of presents unless it was Christmas or a birthday—I was placed in a position of now having to see him as a deadbeat dad and I had just met him. How short-lived was this moment of joy? The pressure was so great from my mother, who was only concerned about her relationship with my stepfather from whom she was separated at the time, that I felt the need to make a choice. So, in my young mind I did what I felt I had to do to keep the peace with my mother. I told my newly acknowledged biological father that he could be my friend, but that my stepfather was my dad. It was because of this that my biological father went away forever, though he was still allowed to have a relationship with my brother. So, in my mind, my brother had it all. He, at least, could acknowledge openly who his parents were.

Keep in mind this was around the same time my mother broke the news of her pregnancy. I was still trying to process how that was even possible, since she was separated from my stepfather and we lived in an apartment in which he didn't live. Talk about being perplexed. I had plenty of mixed emotions that I could not describe and no one from whom to seek clarity. The good news in it all was that at least it was time for school to be out for the summer.

My mother and my stepfather were getting back together, there was a new baby on the way, and they bought a house that we moved into before school started. Yet another new address— yippy! Little did I know at the time that the new house would feel more like a place of employment than a home. While I was very excited for the new baby, I very quickly became the live-in babysitter. Not only was I the babysitter, I had to share a room with him. As a 13-year-old, I would fall asleep and wake up to a crib in front of me.

The only thing I looked forward to was going to school. I immersed myself in my schoolwork. However, I was also tasked with taking on plenty of motherly responsibilities as it related to looking after my younger brother, Chris. While I established an unbreakable bond with my adorable little brother, it was not the ideal life for a 13-year-old. I did not get any reinforcement from my grandmother, as I was not able to go to her house on weekends. And even though my studies were going well, I had to downplay my successes because my stepbrother did not achieve the best grades and we could not openly discuss my academic success.

I ultimately graduated from eighth grade with honors and it was a very proud moment for me. I cherish a picture of me with my grandmother, who was still my rock when she could be. Yet, the worst was yet to come.

"Severe persistent trauma experienced during childhood far too often leaves a debilitating imprint in the life of survivors. Trauma can produce lifelong damage to mental and physical health and a myriad of other harmful outcomes. Overcoming these traumas takes deep rooted work. Tracee's remarkable story of strength and resilience is a tremendous testimony to her determination to be defined by the strength of her faith and character rather than the abuse she suffered."

—Karen Hamilton, CEO of Bethanna, a prominent Social Services Agency, inclusive of youth crisis services, foster care and adoption services

Ms. Hamilton's long-tenured career at Bethanna has allowed her to work extensively with youth who are survivors. She sees firsthand the mental, emotional, and physical toll that trauma takes and the work needed to overcome these traumas. The way I reframed this time period in my life continues to be a work in process. My interim reframe was to focus on how I had learned to adapt and create something positive in the relationship with my little brother, which at times could overshadow the monumental responsibilities placed on me at such a young age.

I invite you to take a moment to reflect on any trauma you experienced as an early adolescent. Oftentimes, hearing another person's experiences of trauma can trigger our own stories. Contemplate the things that happened in your life as you were leaving childhood and entering the teenage years and, if you are able, take this opportunity to work openly on reframing those traumas.

A monumental trauma that I need to reframe is:

_____

_____

_____

_____

I make the choice to reframe those memories by restating them in the following way:

_____

_____

_____

_____

I may need to contact the following people to give them an opportunity to understand how I am working through my reframe process:

_____

_____

_____

_____

CHAPTER FOUR

THE CINDERELLA YEARS— COOKING, CLEANING, AND BABYSITTING

Trust given with the wrong motives and in inappropriate circumstances is sure to be deemed a misplaced gamble in the end.

Scenario 1: Picking up Chris from daycare, walking home with him, getting him situated, preparing dinner and having it on the table by the time my parents arrived home. Scenario 2: Watching Chris all day, preparing dinner and having it on the table when my parents came home from work. What part of either of these scenarios should be the routine for a 13-year-old? This was a normal day for me while all my friends were living their lives—having fun riding bikes and hanging around outside. Going to the grocery store periodically was considered normal for a kid my age in the neighborhood I grew up in, but even that normal activity came with trauma. The walk to the grocery store involved walking behind the strip center that housed the market, coming up from the side of the building. The walk was not so much the issue, though it did not compare to the enjoyable walks to the corner store at my grandmother's. In most cases, the walk to the store was just another instance of being assigned to something that took away opportunities to just hang out with my friends and do simple, fun, 13-year-old kid stuff that everyone else in the neighborhood got to do. Nonetheless, what was the likelihood that I would be walking to the store, coming to the point behind the strip center, and a man would pull up in a car and jump out, wearing only a shirt, socks, and shoes, jingling his private parts? My sprinting skills were once again put into action. It seemed so unfair to me; everyone else was out playing, but I felt constantly under threat and needing to run for my life.

When I was "off duty," and my parents came home, I still did not feel like I was released for the day. The reins on me were so tight compared to my older brother; he was free to go and come as he pleased, but not me. Once school started, I did have the opportunity to return to the one thing that was a constant in my life: going to Public School #26, which was across the street from Grandma's house. Going to school each day placed me in the vicinity of where I found the most joy in my life. I had thrived academically through junior high, my seventh and eighth grade years. I was also a cheerleader, played basketball, and ran track—I was a natural with plenty of sprinting experience. All these activities were introduced to me at the recreation center run by my grandfather. The common theme up to this point in my life was that all positive memories led back to my grandparents.

At the ripe age of 13 going on 14 and having graduated from my K-8 school with honors with my grandmother cheering me on, I was now preparing to spend my whole summer… babysitting. Though my mother was physically in my life, the person who had shown me support, love, and encouragement was my grandmother. One extremely standout recollection throughout my childhood, however, was the work ethic set forth by my mother. She never missed work and we never missed school; therefore, I was certain that I would not be able to miss a day of babysitting during my summer.

Shortly after my graduation from eighth grade, I learned that I would be going to high school on the west side of town, though I lived on the east side. This was actually a good thing, as the high school my older brother attended, which was my parents' alma mater, was considered to be pretty rough because it was attended by all the neighborhood kids who came from our area, which was considered one of the worst parts of the city. The thought never entered my mind that it was going to be even harder to spend time with the one support system that I had depended on all my life. Nonetheless, I was more equipped for my journey to a predominantly white high school as a result of the strong sense of self confidence that was instilled in me by my grandmother, as well as the fact that I quietly thought all white people were poor. I never had any anxiety, trepidation, or concern at this point in my life because I had lived through a period of desegregation in the public schools during which all the white people who were bused to my school were from the worst neighborhoods. This left my naïve, elementary school self with the belief that the less fortunate white people bused to my predominantly African American school were the ultimate representation of the white race. This far-from-the-truth belief kept me from ever feeling inferior of any person throughout my life.

However, this self-confidence could not fill the space in my heart that was becoming ever present for a desire to be wanted, adored, and appreciated—and not just from Grandma. Barry didn't seem to have this problem as he was always "boo-lovin'" with one girlfriend or another, and no one seemed to take issue with that. I, on the other hand, was under lock and key to remain a perpetual child and to carry myself like one. So much so, that I finally wore my first pair of nude panty hose at 13. Up until this point I had to wear white stockings no matter what color outfit I had on. Go figure. Yikes.

So, with the need to feel wanted and babysitting being the highlight of my life, it was only natural that the first boy to show me some attention was who I fell head over heels for. It just happened to be Barry's friend, Larry. My brother did not object because Larry was the least cool of all his friends, so in his mind he was deemed harmless. Larry being labeled my boyfriend was also a non-issue because the closest I got to entertaining him was on the front porch. There was truly a double standard as my brother had girlfriends from the time he was in junior high. It was talked about in the normal course of conversation, yet I was not given any leeway. So, I took what

I could get. By day, I was Cinderella and by evening, I was the undercover porch girlfriend whose beau had to go home by sunset. I did not have a ton of time to have a lot of friends, though I had a few. From time-to-time I was allowed to ride mopeds and go skating with my friends, with many rules and regulations placed on me—totally opposite the lack of parameters placed on Barry.

I was grateful for summer coming to an end, for having survived the summer of babysitting and for preparing to head to high school. There must have been a promise of babysitting pay that I would be required to use to buy essentials that most kids' parents paid for, but it must have been so insignificant that I can't recall what I even bought with the money other than snacks at the Clark gas station that I walked to each day. When high school began, I took three city buses to get to school each morning, but I never complained. I made many new friends—most notably my friend of a lifetime, Michelle—and was academically successful through my freshmen year, though I was still required to go straight home each day and get dinner prepared before everyone else got home to eat at 5:30. I maintained my limited relationship with Larry and even got to my Grandma's house from time-to-time to spend the weekend. Amazingly, I even successfully tried out for the majorette team to become a pom-pom girl for my sophomore year. I was on cruise control at this point; however, there was still the lack of connection between me and my mother. But there were enough distractions for me to be okay with that. I shared the game schedule with my mother so she could come and see me during the half-time show. Her blunt response was that she would only come to one game because she had only gone to one of Barry's games. Wow, that was so supportive. All I could understand was that my parents worked Monday through Friday, evenings and weekends were free, and we had a car. There was no reason for her not to come and see me perform. My only conclusion was that, yet again, I was not a priority. I don't know why I was surprised as this was the same mother who never went to church with us, but instead dropped us off and went back home. Thank goodness the church was only one city block from my grandmother's house—who did not go either but had lunch ready for us by the time church let out. Like most of our other activities, church was spearheaded by our grandfather, who did attend with us each week.

As the perpetual saga of trauma continued, it was about to get very interesting that summer. The trade-off for having to babysit Chris instead of hanging out with my friends, was that my porch boyfriend could now come into the house to keep me company. Sounds a little self-serving for my parents, huh? Of course, we did not mind at all. As an adult with children, I now see the blatant misplacement of trust. While my mother and stepfather were off having a good time, I was at home putting my little brother to sleep, playing house, getting all the affection that I was so starved for, not to mention losing my virginity at 15. I was not a "fast" girl. After all, at this point Larry had been my porch boyfriend for almost two years before he graduated to being welcomed to come into the house and stay with me while I babysat. Giving the space and time on a regular basis, and no supervision to two teenagers who consider themselves boyfriend and girlfriend was a recipe for misplaced intimacy, not misplaced trust. The whole set-up was more about convenience for my parents than actual trust in me. Of course, Barry had been having serious girlfriends regularly since he was in junior high school with no issues from my parents at all. This was indicative of the double-standard. Though not the typical life of a 15-year-old, it was my life and at that point I was okay with it as I was experiencing pure, joyous puppy love.

Though I didn't have the opportunity to be a typical social teen, I did hang with some kids in the neighborhood. I would ride motorized bikes, play cards, and sometimes just sit around and girl talk with a few of the sets of sisters who lived nearby. But I somehow always seemed to be reprimanded even for that kind of innocent fun. While the physical abuse should have been waning, there were still episodes of busted lips and bruises. I was merely riding mopeds with my friends one afternoon and as soon as I checked in, which I thought was the right thing to do, even though it was still light outside, my mother stood at the front door and hit me so hard on the side of my face and head that I had ringing in my ear for several minutes. Her ranting began and all she could do was go on and on about how I did not check in often enough, though that was not established in advance. It was all made better though because I was going to babysit, and I would get to see the one person who I felt cared for me other than my grandmother: my puppy love boyfriend.

My life at 15 was so filled with overwhelming emotion, trauma, and the need to just feel wanted. My summer ended on a sad note because my life's protector, Barry, left to go to college. I was devastated. Though it was a major accomplishment, and I was happy for him, it was a time when I realized life without him at home would never be the same. Who would ultimately be there for me?

That same summer I turned 16 and was on a mission to get a real job: I started working at McDonald's. I received my first paycheck and life was good. I went to work, went to school, babysat Chris, and "played house" with my boyfriend while my parents went out on the weekends. School was back in session and it was about to go to the next level. Larry and I decided to "play house" on a day when school was not in session. Chris was in daycare, Barry was off at college, I do not recall where my stepbrother was, and I thought my parents were at work. I called Larry over. He arrived jolly on the spot. We went to my room for the first time; we normally played house on the back porch. It seemed that as soon as we got comfortable, we heard the front door open. The front door was just down the stairs from my room. Larry jumped in the closet and I pretended to be asleep. My stepfather opened my door and firmly asked, "Where is he?" I didn't know that dumb Larry had driven his mother's car and parked it in front of the house. I had assumed that he rode his bike, which was his normal mode of transportation. My stepfather left the room and said Larry better get out immediately. He rushed out and boy was I embarrassed! It did not matter that my boyfriend had been caught in my room; I just knew this was on the road to total disaster once my mother came home. I was not mistaken. While I thought my mother had called me every name in the book, now "whore" was neatly added to the list. My world was shattered, I was on punishment, and all I could do from then on was go to work, go to school, and babysit. The most challenging of all was that without my boyfriend, I had no one to affirm me or make me feel wanted because I did not have a lot of time with my grand-mother due to work, school, and babysitting. I felt so lost.

"Raising daughters is a challenge and a blessing. Not only did I raise three daughters, but from the ages of 6, 12, and 15, I raised them alone after a divorce from their father. He had no interest in them after exiting the marriage and I knew what I had to. It was important for me that I remain honest with them, give them encouragement constantly, and provide as many opportunities as I could manage so they could make positive decisions for their lives.

"My daughters are very successful women now (ages 35, 40, and 42). One is a breast cancer surgeon, one is a VP for HBO, and the youngest is a senior art director for Target. Life is a journey and has bumps along the way, but you, the parent, must be the role model and mentor for your children. I could not let my pain be a part of how I would raise my children. This is my advice for mothers who are raising their babies."

—Dr. Naomi Booker, Educator and CEO of Charter Schools

As a lifelong educator and current CEO of charter schools, Dr. Booker points out the importance of being a role model for your own children—no matter what trauma you have endured yourself. Being the single mother to three daughters also gives her a unique perspective on how to mother girls to be independent, successful women. I did not have this kind of example in my life as a teenager. I am not excusing my behavior but giving myself permission to realize that I was nothing more than a teenage girl with raging hormones who was lacking a true male figure that provided love and affirmation. I had to reframe being made to feel like I was a whore, and slut, as my mother characterized me, to one of a misguided teenager searching to replicate the feelings of love and affection that had only been bestowed upon me by my grandmother. I did not give myself a pass for disrespecting my mother's house, no matter who else did as it still was not appropriate but given the circumstances of being given the time and space, I was no worse than any other teen who had done the same thing, they just did not get caught.

I invite you to take a moment to reflect on any trauma you experienced as a teenager. Oftentimes, hearing another person's experiences of trauma can trigger our own stories. Contemplate the things that happened in your life during high school and, if you are able, please work openly on reframing those traumas.

A period of overwhelming trauma during my teen years that I need to reframe is:

_____

_____

_____

_____

I make the choice to reframe this period by restating it in the following way:

_____

_____

_____

_____

CHAPTER FIVE

THERE WAS NOTHING SWEET ABOUT 16

Children are the products of their environment;
they don't do what you say, they do what they see.

"Sweet 16" was not how I associated my 16th year. I was going to school, working, and babysitting. After the big bust, for lack of a better way to describe it, I was merely existing. My mother reiterated the speech of how I should be abstaining from sex and waiting until I was married. This was the ideal thing to say, but not the practical thing to say. Given all that I had been exposed to in my young life, I had never been shown the example of abstinence. Don't get me wrong, I know it is right to want more for your child than you had, but at the stage that it was obvious I was no longer a virgin, the talk was a moot point. I was not offered birth control, but instead preached to about abstaining.

November of that year, my mother picked me up from my job at McDonald's, looked me up and down, and blatantly said, "I think you are pregnant." I knew I was gaining weight, but because I never had a regular menstrual cycle, the thought that I might be pregnant never crossed my mind. I was eating a lot of McDonald's food too. My mother quickly arranged for me to go to the doctor. She did not take me herself—it must have been too embarrassing for her—but instead enlisted my uncle's girlfriend to take me. The doctor confirmed the news: I was 16 and pregnant. Who would have thought that they would have a TV show today glamourizing that of which I was so ashamed? And the news was even worse than that. Where I am certain, if it were possible, I would have been signed up for an abortion, it was too late! It is real—there is such a thing as the power of suppression. I was seven months pregnant and did not recall one bit of the overall gestational process up to that point. I still was not really showing, other than a slight pooch instead of my normally flat stomach. This meant that my mother had to think fast—and that she did. Within a couple days, I was escorted to an adoption agency where it was all arranged for a very nice couple to adopt my unborn child. I was so disconnected that none of it mattered to me. My mother notified my now ex-boyfriend's parents, so that he could sign over his rights, and the process was underway for me to bring forth a child for a deserving family to raise.

I was able to work for another month after learning I was pregnant. I wore the same jacket to school each day so that no one could notice my changing shape. I never actually got big enough that it was obvious that I was pregnant, although some may have suspected that something was going on under that jacket. I should have saved it as a souvenir as it was the ultimate disguise. By December, I was so sad and lonely—I could not see my grandparents for fear that they would know I was expecting. For Christmas I was given a sewing machine, which was nice because I loved to sew. The only patterns that I was given, however, were for making night gowns because I was an outcast and pregnant. I remember the nice lady, who must have been the social worker from the adoption agency, picking me up from school for my monthly doctor's appointments in December and January. My mother never went with me to any prenatal appointments at all. After she made the arrangements for the adoption, she distanced herself from any further involvement. I continued my routine of going to school, coming home, doing my chores, and cooking or getting dinner started as I always did during the week. This was a very telling time for me as it relates to my high school best girlfriend, Michelle. She never knew how much her friendship meant to me back then. I do not know if she had any inkling of what was going on with me. If she did, she never said a mumbling word. She just kept being my friend, laughing and teasing me every day about being "sew perfect,"—we were in sewing class together. To this day, she has such an unconditional love for me, and I truly feel blessed for that.

Michelle was the first of a group of true friends who would come to collectively be known as my Fab 5 girlfriends. These female friendships showed me how important it is to surround yourself with people who have your best interests at heart.

Each one of them is significant. After Michelle, Torrye, who happened to be from neighboring Chicago even though we met in New Jersey, became the next significant friendship for me. She was the first friend who shared my true love for retail therapy. Our weekly shopping trips created a bond that we share even today. I also met Sheila in New Jersey. Sheila played many roles in addition to being Godmother for both my children. Sheila, along with my husband, was along for the journey in the early stages of my recognizing and reframing my trauma. She has occupied the role of surrogate mother, sister, friend, and devil's advocate, whether asked or not. Her willingness to just be and listen with such compassion and encouragement has been my lifeline on so many occasions.

The fourth of my Fab 5 is Kelli, who has been more of a little sister, as she often conveys how much she has gained by just being with me and learning so many lessons. Her willingness to be there throughout the years created an imprint on my heart and sealed her fate as one of my Fab 5. The last of my Fab 5, but certainly in no way the least, is Beth. Beth is my feisty and fun-loving friend who is always there for me to wind down with and just be myself. Each one of my Fab 5 is amazing in her own right and I am extremely thankful for them. None of our friendships have gone without being challenged in some way, whether big or small, but we have loved each other through it all. Each, in her own special way, made me feel important and loved, just as my beloved grandmother had done. They taught me that I was capable and able to love other females, not just my grandmother.

All that being said, even with having an amazing friendship with Michelle and her being a bright spot in my life, it all came to a head when I went into labor on a Friday afternoon after school (how convenient). I had the baby naturally with no medication—when asked, my mother told them not to give me any so that I could feel the pain—and was back in school on Monday morning. I never held the baby that I was told was a boy, which may be why I never had any form of separation anxiety. It was a totally closed adoption and I was okay with that. I was confident that the child was going to a much better family than the one I could provide. I can truly say I experienced the power of suppression as it was what I did unconsciously throughout the pregnancy and delivery.

At that juncture, I felt renewed. I went to school on that Monday with my head high. I was instructed to wear the pregnancy concealing jacket that I had been wearing, so that it would not be obvious that something had changed since Friday. Of course, I left the house with the jacket on, but was anxious to show off my perfectly flat stomach that I had lost during my pregnancy. I remember my outfit very vividly. I had on a crisp button-down light blue shirt with pleats. I had it tucked into some nicely fitted Gloria Vanderbilt jeans with my caramel-colored belt and caramel-colored medium heeled shoes. The added bonus in my mind was that even though I had been given the medication to dry-up my milk glands after giving birth, my bust-line was quite nice. Especially given that I had always been known for a nice butt and not necessarily boobs. On this day I had both, and I was determined to take that jacket off, if only for a short while. I took the jacket off and strutted down the hallway with massive confidence, only to turn the corner toward my locker and looking down, I saw a huge wet spot on my shirt where I must have had leakage—after all, it was only the third day after giving birth. Thank God I was close to my locker where my jacket hung. I could not spin my locker combination fast enough. Not wearing the jacket was a blessing in disguise because if I had worn the jacket, it also would have been wet. Talk about being saved by the bell. That experience was very humbling for me. Needless to say, I don't think I took the jacket off for the next two weeks. I was ashamed and shamed, but I could now go visit my grandmother, which was nourishment to my soul.

"Imagine being a vulnerable young girl, tormented for years with assaults on your worth, stability, and self-esteem; made to feel disgusting; and abandoned because of the life growing within you. Voiceless, subjected to constant messages of shame, numb from incredible pressure to maintain the appearance of life with no change, and ultimately being faced with the choice of adoption. Fortunately for Tracee and her unborn child, she had the instinct to know that adoption opened up possibilities and hope for a baby she would never know, and for whom she was in no position to provide for. I have personally witnessed this as the story of far too many young girls, yet in many cases they do not even recognize adoption as a viable option to give a young life opportunity that they just cannot provide."

—Karen Hamilton, CEO of Bethanna, a prominent Social Services Agency, inclusive of youth crisis services, foster care and adoption services

As Ms. Hamilton states, the adoption process creates overwhelming feelings for all parties involved. As the mother giving her baby up for adoption, I knew I was doing the best for that life and am grateful that was an option for me. The reframe for this dramatic and emotional time in my life caused much reflection. It allowed me to recognize that though my mother may not have been nurturing, loving, or affectionate, she did not want me to suffer the perpetual trauma of being a teen parent struggling to raise a child. For this, I am forever grateful. While many people have struggled and kept their children, I say God Bless You—that is not the plan God had for my life. I am very thankful that my mother, for whatever reason—perhaps to save face for herself and to help me—made the most critical and pivotal decision along my life's path toward the person and the life I have today.

I encourage you to take a moment to reflect on any trauma you experienced as an older teenager. Oftentimes, hearing another person's experiences of trauma can trigger our own stories. Contemplate on the things that happened during your later teen years and, if you are able, feel free to work openly on reframing those traumas.

A trauma that was pivotal during my later teen years that I need to reframe is:

_____

_____

_____

_____

I make the choice to reframe this trauma by restating it in the following way:

_____

_____

_____

_____

CHAPTER SIX

"TIME AIN'T LONG
AS IT HAS BEEN"

Consider every step and misstep
as one toward a greater outcome,
even when the path seems unclear.

I was now past one of the most challenging times in my life as a young girl. I was still in the second semester of my junior year of high school and had retired the infamous jacket. Spring was starting and I was getting over my first boyfriend; I was required to break up with him as part of my ultimate punishment. What was not taken into consideration was that I was still a teenage girl who was desirable to the boys at my school. The only reason I never liked or even noticed any of them was because I had my boyfriend. Well now, it was fair game. By April of my junior year, I had a new boyfriend, who my mother professed to like at the time. I was automatically going to be his prom date, which is what we did back then. There were no "promposals." I was a superb seamstress and if it were ever in question, one could just ask Michelle. Also, if I were going to prom, there was only one way I could have a prom dress—I would make it myself, and so I did. I chose one of the hardest designs by Vogue, which was meant to be a wedding dress—maybe that was a sign of things to come. I even made it in white. Later, I learned that my Fab 5 friend, Sheila, and I had the same taste even before we knew each other. She had the same dress made for her actual wedding—how ironic.

My prom was amazing. I had the normal cast of characters to see me off: my mother, father, brother Chris, and uncle. During my teen years, prom night was somewhat of a rite of passage. It was the first time we could stay out all night. I know for a fact that my brother, Barry, went to a hotel after each of his prom nights, so why shouldn't I do the same? Well, we did. It was a magical night—for what I knew to be magical at that age—and it was almost weird as there were not a lot of questions when we returned the next morning. It was as though no one wanted to put us in the position to have to lie. Thank goodness!

As glorious as that day was, the daily routine set in shortly after: chores and babysitting. However, at this point I was still working my job at McDonald's and had my own money for the most part. I spent as much time as I could with my boyfriend. He was also a huge help in that he had access to his mother's car and gave me rides home from work. Disagreements continued between my mother and me, but that was normal for any teen girl and her mother. The difference for me was how explosive they were. It seemed like every situation had to result in an all-out attack. I remember there was always a lesson in everything. It would have been okay if every lesson did not have to be learned in such a drastic, dogmatic way. I remember having a barrette in my hair that I got from a friend. To teach me the lesson not to share personal items with others, my mother asked for the barrette and broke it, so that I would have to replace it. Yes, the lesson was learned, but why so drastically was the question. To teach me to keep my dresser drawers neat, if one thing was out of place, the entire drawer was thrown out onto the floor and I had to refold everything. These types of lessons spanned from overall hygiene to ensuring that my nail polish was not chipped. It instilled a sense of excellence and resentment all at the same time.

As the summer approached between my junior and senior year of high school, I remember the never-ending battles over every little thing. It got so bad that my mother put me out. I was big and bad, and I left and moved in with my two cousins, who were only one and two years older than me. They had their own apartment since their mother had died and left them on their own. Living with them gave me a sense of freedom I had longed for without constant bickering and complaining. My mother and I really had no communication for the month and a half that I lived with my cousins.

I continued with my same boyfriend, and we could come and go as we pleased. It was fine except for two major drawbacks: I had to sleep on the couch and the apartment had roaches. I had never lived with roaches before and after six weeks I had all I could take. I packed up my one suitcase and headed home. I was allowed back, but my mother made me unpack my suitcase on the front porch. Once home, the drama picked up right where it left off. I was constantly reminded of how my mother "held the key." Added to that, I had another pregnancy scare in my senior year of high school. It turned out to be a condition called amenorrhea, and it would be something I struggled with through my adult life.

But senior year was not all bad. I secured my next job, which was at the hardware store and paid more, and I sat on a stool at the cash register ringing up purchases. I was also at the top of my class, ranking 27 out of a class of 550, and a member of the National Honor Society. These were things that most people aspired to have, yet came easy for me, and the natural progression would have been to go to college.

But instead of college, I decided it was better for me to marry my high school sweetheart and get out of my mother's house. Sure, I loved my boyfriend, but he was also my ticket to a new life. I can vividly recall my mother standing on the step, looking at him, and saying "You f...d up my daughter's life." Regardless of my mother's reaction, he was my invisible lifeline to anything outside of Indianapolis.

My boyfriend turned husband was enlisted in the military, which meant my high school sweetheart husband (HSSH) and I were headed to New Jersey. He left before I did, and I had to bear five months before I was able to leave. I thought the trauma would subside. At this point, I had a job at one of the top banks in Indianapolis as a bank teller and customer service representative, and I worked there until it was time for me to leave.

I spent as much time as possible with my grandmother during those months. One of my fondest memories was when I got my new personal checking account and wrote my first check to my grandmother out of pure excitement for writing a real check made payable to someone—who better than to my "bestie" grandmother. The check was for $10—and she cashed it. During this period, my HSSH was away at basic training and then his military job training, and I was dealing with all the negativity at home on my own. I recall my grandmother always telling me, "time ain't long as it has been." This meant that with each passing day, there was less time until I could leave. I will never forget the last beating I suffered at the hands of my mother. I was told to pay the phone bill at the bank where I worked. It was my understanding that I had to pay my portion, which was always very high. I had no idea that there was an impending shut-off notice. I paid my portion, thinking that was all that was expected of me. But because the balance of the bill was not paid, the phone was cut off. I remember my mother screaming at me, following me down the walkway in the back of the house, and ultimately tackling me to the ground, beating me. It was so bad that my dad came out of the garage and yelled at her to get off me. The next day the phone bill was paid, and the phone was back on. The memory of the beating will never be erased. She beat me like I was a rabid dog on the street, and I could not fight back.

I was able to seek refuge with my grandmother, who reminded me that "time ain't long as it has been."

This was another reframe where I had to really sort out how I felt. Still not understanding how my mother may have been feeling or what motivated her, I had to reach the conclusion that if I minimized it, I would continue to rationalize it instead of being healed from it. I had to recognize that no matter what may have happened to my mother, it still did not make what she did to me okay. I had to make the conscious decision to simply focus on forgiveness. I recognized that forgiveness was more for me than for her, and it allowed me to regain power over my feelings and outcomes. I had to see it as another opportunity to overcome in the face of adversity.

I invite you to take a moment to reflect on any trauma where you had to forgive simply for your own well-being. Oftentimes, hearing another person's experiences of trauma can trigger our own stories. Contemplate on things that happened that you had to forgive and, if you are able, feel free to work openly on reframing those traumas.

A trauma that challenged me to focus on forgiveness was:

_____

_____

_____

_____

I make the choice to reframe this trauma by restating it in the following way:

_____

_____

_____

_____

CHAPTER SEVEN

GETTING OUT OF DODGE

It's not what we see, but how we view it.

The day finally came when I was boarding a plane and leaving the city. On one hand, I felt scared; on the other hand, I felt a sense of security. I was like a caged bird being set free. For the first time, I was not going to be under the controlling thumb of a mother who was consumed with proving that she was in total control and that "she held the key." For the first time, I felt like I could figuratively take the key and throw it away.

I got off the plane in Philadelphia as it was the closest airport to where I would be living in New Jersey. I was amazed that, for the first time in my life, I was not in Indiana and was only responsible for myself—no babysitting and no one with a never-ending opinion of everything I did. It very quickly became apparent just how sheltered and limited my environment had been in Indiana. I vividly recall looking at several people who did not appear to be either white or black. My HSSH met me at the arrival gate and I immediately asked, "What kind of people are they?" My HSSH's military companion who gave him a ride to pick me up replied, "You have never seen a Hispanic person before?" I said obviously not, we did not have those kinds of people in Indiana. Talk about being sheltered and not exposed. I went on to say that in Indiana, people were either white or black. He was just as surprised by the fact that I had never seen a Hispanic person as I was in seeing one for the first time.

I was happier than I had been in a long time. We headed to military housing for couples where we were staying until we were assigned housing of our own. It took about two or three long weeks, but who was counting? We quickly settled into our substandard military housing that was amazing to us because we could begin our grown-up lives and not have to answer to anyone but ourselves. I began experiencing life as a military wife. It came natural to me as I had spent so much time cooking and cleaning at my mother's house, and I fell into a domesticated flow without even thinking about it. There was really no adjustment period, and I was still a teenager. But there were many young couples just like us. One major difference, though, was that we did not have any kids and were not planning or expecting any. I quickly learned that many of the young women were quite content being married to a military man, living in free military housing, having babies, collecting the monthly pay and benefits, and going to the commissary. This was not my story to tell. I got a full-time job at a local bank and quickly hit the resume button on my life as an independent young woman with her own money.

I missed my grandmother immensely and had to admit that no matter how dysfunctional the relationship may have been, I missed my mother a little as well. My lifeline continued to be my grandmother as she wrote and called with her comedic neighborhood updates quite often. For the most part, my mother and I only spoke when I called, which continues to this day. This really did not matter though. I was so homesick by the holidays that it did not matter who called; any familiar voice on the other end of the phone was all I longed for.

I arrived in November and adjusted to my new life in our one-bedroom apartment. It was so small that the refrigerator did not fit in the kitchen but was in the corner of the dining room. I met two of my dearest friends who are now in my Fab 5 group within six months of each other. I first met Torrye, who was active-duty military and the choir director at the chapel on the military base. We quickly became quite close. She was a true fashionista when not in uniform. I was able to spend my money the way I wanted, and we established a Bamberger's (now Macy's) ritual where we shopped on Saturdays for our Sunday church outfits. My additional ritual was to stop at the Non-Commissioned Officers (NCO) Club in between. I would party at the NCO club on Saturday night and sing in the choir on Sunday morning—I had balance for a young person. Torrye was always honest with me and never failed to remind me that

I was not a soloist, but I was a good choir soprano. I told her that God knew what not to give me—big boobs and an amazing voice as they both would have been misused.

Soon after, I met Sheila, who moved in across the walkway from me and had the identical apartment to mine. We also quickly hit it off, with a love for fashion being a big thing we had in common as well. We also were in tune to ensure that we kept our apartments nice for our young military husbands. The key difference between us was how noticeable it was to me that she and her husband were very much in love, while I was beginning to recognize how my young marriage was quickly becoming a routine.

Eight months passed, it was summer in New Jersey, and I looked forward to a visit from my grandmother and little brother, Chris. It quickly became apparent that I was merely a babysitter, as my mother and stepfather drove the 12 hours from Indianapolis to drop off my grandmother and Chris for a two-week visit, but they had no intention of spending any time with me before getting back on the road. If they had vacation time, it clearly was not going to be spent with me in New Jersey. I'm certain they rationalized that they would see me when we drove Grandma and Chris back to Indianapolis after their two-week visit. I can't say there was any real disappointment as my grandmother was as loving as she had always been. She watched Chris while I worked and she played dress-up in my shoes and clothes—we wore the same size—until I got home. She cooked all the meals that I missed, we went to the boardwalk, and she was able to get in her nips of her gin with water chaser. Grandma was a hit with all our friends and was unforgettable. Before you knew it, the time had come to drive them back to Indiana. I traveled back to Indianapolis with my HSSH, my grandmother, and Chris. It was an uneventful trip, which is likely the best of all possible scenarios, and I enjoyed some shopping and getting reacquainted with some of my favorite Indy foods like rib tips and fish platters—they are just not the same in New Jersey. While I always liked New Jersey, I was never fond of goodbyes, and leaving Indianapolis always proved difficult—even leaving my mother. Most of all, leaving Grandma always created a hole in my heart.

My marriage to my HSSH was regular at best. I operated in a manner that I was taught during my Cinderella years. I kept a clean house and kept the refrigerator full. I cooked dinner on a regular basis, ensured that I kept up my appearance, and submitted to what I thought was a healthy sexual relationship—fortunately, I learned later what I was missing. After all, that was the only blueprint I had seen for a marriage. Never mind that passion, a sense of longing, support, and fun were not present. It was not until I became close friends with Sheila that I realized just how unfulfilled I was in my young marriage. I had the opportunity to witness what real love looked like in her marriage to her husband, Donnie. They were truly a happy newlywed couple, full of love and adoration for one another. So, I worked, hung out, went to church, and stayed in close contact with my grandmother. I had the phone bills to prove it.

A huge highlight during this time was to take every opportunity to serve as a third wheel with Sheila and Donnie on their trips to New York City, which was their hometown. The opportunity to experience NYC with natives was a blast. While many people want to see Times Square, that was not my desire. Coming from the inner city, I wanted to see the worst parts of New York to compare them to the worst part of Indianapolis. Donnie and Sheila made my wish come true by driving me through Hunts Point, an area known for prostitution. I was left in utter amazement at the streetwalkers who did not bother to wear anything significant on their bottom half. A G-string and a coat were the order of the night. I think I talked about that for a very long time. This could not be characterized as trauma, but instead self-inflicted adventure, as I was safely with my friends. I felt no guilt in leaving my HSSH behind to his favorite pastime—basketball—as we merely maintained a basic marriage of work Monday through Friday, I cooked and cleaned, and we did whatever we wanted to do otherwise.

I found a level of friendship and connection with Sheila that I had never experienced before. She served as a friend, confidant, mother-figure—she was older than me—and my licensed beautician. Talk about having a complete package. She gave meaning to the word full-cycle, as she was truly a full-cycle friend. She was so supportive and helpful. We could always tell each other anything and would do anything for each other. One of our more unforgettable moments was when she was putting a perm in my hair and she went into labor. My first response was to confirm that she was going to finish my hair, to which she replied, "Yes!" You might be saying that it seemed selfish on my part, but I did hang in there with her and Donnie in final preparations, all the way to the hospital, and through the night. I finally went home in the early morning; shortly after, her baby boy was born. I was almost there for the birth. I believe I paid my dues for that perm. And I would not change a thing as it is one of my most memorable moments.

During my second summer in Jersey, I would have been excited for the impending visit by Grandma. But that summer my grandmother was not coming. It did not, however, stop my mother from bringing Chris. And again, it was only a drop off with no time for a visit between my mother and me. This was an opportunity for my "bestie" Sheila to come through for me in another form. She now had her firstborn and was available to babysit Chris while I went to work each day. I needed to save my vacation for when we drove back to Indianapolis to take Chris back home.

I greatly anticipated this trip back to Indianapolis as I could not wait to spend time with my grandmother. The visit went well, but as always, seemed all too short. But this time, I was not plagued with the normal sadness and anxiety of leaving as I was planning to return the next month to be in a friend's wedding. Between the two summer visits I discovered a new song by Diane Reeves called, "Better Days." It conveyed the love that the singer/songwriter had for her grandmother, just like the unwavering love I had for my mine. I went with my mother to my grandmother's house with the cassette tape and recording in hand to play and sing to my grandmother. It did not matter that I had to use a little cassette tape player with the speaker on top, it served its purpose. By singing the song, I was able to convey to my grandmother that she was and had been the biggest inspiration in my life. I was not concerned how this was perceived by my mother as she stood and witnessed this ultimate display of affection between my grandmother and me. The song was about the love for a grandmother that had passed away. Little did I know at the time that this would be one of the last visits that I would have with my grandmother. My mother informed me that my grandmother was being treated for throat cancer. I cannot recall if this was the reason that she did not visit me earlier that summer in New Jersey; however, it was apparent that she was not fully herself. I remember always making it a point to spend the night with my grandmother whenever I was home, but on this visit for the wedding, it was such a quick trip that I did not have time to stay at Grandma's. The evening before I was set to fly back to New Jersey, my grandfather stopped by with Grandma in the passenger seat of the car. I leaned in the car to give my grandmother hugs and kisses. It was the last time I felt her touch, smelled her scent, and kissed her sweet, fragile face.

I flew back to New Jersey to prepare for the next significant shift in my life: my HSSH was being sent on a tour of duty to Korea for a one-year assignment. While leaving my grandmother behind to return to New Jersey prompted feelings of deep despair and anxiety, my HSSH leaving for a year was not particularly monumental or emotion filled. We would be separated for a year and it would prove to open my eyes to the realities of our marriage. He did not feel it necessary to spend the evening before he was scheduled to leave for Korea with me. At this point, the writing was on the wall for me, it was over. He left in September and my life carried on as usual, except I had no responsibility to cook and be a wife in a lackluster marriage. I had no one to take care of and was living out the teenage years I never got to experience as an actual teenager. For a short while, all was humming along with me going to work, hanging out, and singing in the military base chapel choir with Torrye as the choir director.

In November of that year, Barry, who happened to be stationed at the same base, and I received news that our grandmother was not doing well and probably would not make it. Up to this point, my brother and I were able to keep in contact, though our lives were clearly very different. He was a single soldier, and I was living the married life. However, we came together instantly and immediately got on the road to Indianapolis. Instead of going directly to Grandma's house, we were instructed to meet at my mother's house. We arrived there by the evening of the following day. We were told to sit on the sofa and my mother broke the news that we had not made it in time to say goodbye to our grandmother. Grandma had passed away. I remember letting out a loud cry, only to be told by my mother in her normal, controlling, intimidating, and firm tone, to be quiet before I woke up my little brother. All I could think was, "I can't even grieve without being told how to do that to her liking?" The funeral and wake were all taken care of by my grandfather, and I would assume with the help of my mother and uncle. I had never attended any form of homegoing services before then, let alone a wake and funeral for the person

I loved most in this world. I could never convey this for fear of further rejection by my mother. I felt the epitome of loneliness and did not know where to turn.

For a short period, I was open to thinking that maybe my dull and lifeless marriage might be salvaged as my HSSH offered his condolences from afar and I was very receptive given the level of numbness I felt. When I went back to New Jersey, I was all alone except for Sheila and her cute little family, although they were preparing to leave for a three-year assignment in Germany. I was about to really be all alone. I loved Barry, but we did not have much reason or opportunity to cross paths on the base.

The trauma of loneliness became very real to me. My coping mechanism for it was to work and party, work and party. I did not get any level of additional support from my mother during what was probably a very difficult time for her as well. Nonetheless, I was the one in a state far away and all alone. I guess I should not have expected anything different. This was just another confirmation of not being important enough, which to me was another form of rejection.

This mundane existence carried on through a mid-term visit from my HSSH. This visit only confirmed that the marriage really was over. Before he could return, I sent the Dear John letter and checked out of the marriage mentally and physically for good. Even with all the rejection from my mother, I still felt the need to have her support of my decision to get a divorce. I am certain that it had a lot to do with my family, especially my grandfather who did not believe in divorce.

I recall saying to her, "The rest of my life is a long time to live unhappy."

This was an extremely low point in my life. However, I made the conscious decision to stay in New Jersey and go it on my own. I was working full-time on the military base as a full-charge bookkeeper and office manager with full profit and loss (P&L) responsibility, which I attribute to much of my success today. I made what would be considered well beyond a life-sustaining wage for a single person. My high-level math aptitude served me well. With that, I had no desire to return to Indiana and end up back under my mother's fear-provoking, intimidating, and controlling thumb. I was not certain of what I wanted, but I was sure that if I returned to Indianapolis, I would not be happy. I felt as though I would just get sucked back into supporting my mother's agenda, especially given that Chris was only eight years old at the time. I was determined to take this opportunity to show that I could make something of myself that was contrary to what my mother had always said. I knew that it was my time to take control of the reigns and forge a life for myself—no mother, no husband, no baby brother. I was going to take care of me. I stayed extremely focused, though I grieved my grandmother daily and had separation anxiety from Sheila, who now lived in another country. I enrolled in college and maintained my full-time employment, working for a government contractor on the military base. I lived in military housing until my HSSH returned from Korea, at which time he returned to the barracks since getting back together was not an option.

Ultimately, my Uncle Henry co-signed with me on my first apartment. I never missed a rent payment and to this day have never missed a mortgage payment either. I can hear him vividly saying to never get behind, "because if you can't pay one payment, you surely can't pay two."

Divorce was imminent at this point, so I did not bother providing my soon-to-be ex with my phone number or address. I was happy to move on and look toward better things ahead— life could only go up from there. Even with this persevering perspective, there was now the trauma that would come with the label of being divorced.

"Right before I married my ex-husband, I remember my mother saying to me, 'I don't see any passion between the two of you.' To which I flippantly responded, 'we have sex.' It wasn't until after my ex left that I understood what she meant. I learned two lessons during that time. First, good sex is not the passion that sustains a marriage. The second lesson came during a therapy session, where I realized that there is nothing lonelier than feeling alone in a room with another person. As I sat at that last session, I embraced how liberating it was to live on my own terms. While it was devastating to go through a separation just six weeks after being married, I was not the first woman to go through it and I would not be the last. I was determined that I would be stronger and more prepared for love when it came my way again, and boy was I. Twenty-seven years later and counting, there is nothing sweeter."

—Valerie Cofield, CEO of Eastern Minority Development Council

Ms. Cofield is an inspiration for her willingness to open-up regarding the toll that being young and divorced can have on a person. One's own perspective on a situation has a major role in the positive or negative implications of how that trauma will manifest. The trauma during this period of my life was overwhelming and at times still has a sting. In such a short time frame, and at such a young age, I was faced with continued rejection, loss of a significant loved one, divorce, and loneliness. Attempting to reframe the chain of events that occurred required me to dissect the effects of each individual event. Although my mother did not spend time with me, I was thankful that she at least made possible the visits with my grandmother and little brother. My takeaway from my marriage was that I may not have known what I wanted, but I was very clear about what I did not want. The grief of losing my grandmother challenged me the most. This is where I gained a sense of freedom in recognizing that I truly loved her more than anything in the world and that I had the right to grieve her for as long as it took. I operated from a space of persistence to keep moving forward and to show how I could make something of myself and prove to my mother that I was going to be a success.

I invite you to take a moment to reflect on any trauma that left you wanting to completely give up. Oftentimes, hearing another person's experiences of trauma can trigger our own stories. Contemplate the things that happened that forced you to motivate yourself to move forward and, if you are able, feel free to work openly on reframing those traumas.

I was motivated to reframe this trauma as a result of:

_____

_____

_____

_____

I make the choice to reframe this trauma by restating it in the following way:

_____

_____

_____

_____

CHAPTER EIGHT

TRAUMA IS DIRTY LAUNDRY THAT NEEDS TO BE WASHED, DRIED, AND PUT AWAY

It takes a village, but, be careful
who you allow in the village.

As I continued navigating my early twenties, separated with an impending divorce, I felt free. I masked the loneliness by staying busy, working and taking college classes, and, of course, partying at the NCO clubs on the weekends. I had a decent-paying job and I was adjusting to my new normal. My Uncle Henry and Aunt Mary lived about an hour away, and I now made it a priority to see them on a more regular basis. They were extremely supportive when I shared the news that I was getting divorced and they vowed to be there for whatever I needed. They were truly an inspiration. They were the first couple in my family, outside of my grandparents, that allowed me to see what a happy marriage looked like. Beyond that,

Aunt Mary was a living example of what loving one's daughter as an adult looked like. I recall her saying to me once that she thought it was important for her to send something to her daughter on a regular basis, just because she was her daughter. This was so amazing to me, given that I barely spoke to my mother unless I initiated the call. I was now beginning to unpack all the feelings layered on myself. Instead of perceiving that it was my fault that my mother did not want to be bothered with me, I began to see how important it was for the parent to take the initiative to forge a meaningful relationship with their child. Nonetheless, I was still dealing with the ongoing effects of the trauma of rejection.

Life was moving along in an uneventful way. After all that I had been through, uneventful was a good thing.

It was a Saturday night, and like any Saturday night, I was planning to hang out at the NCO club on the army base. But that night, I was not interested in dressing up with the high heels and a sexy outfit. It was going to be a night with my flat shoes, hair pulled back in a ponytail, and make-up that only consisted of a slither of eyeliner and lip gloss. My girlfriend and I were going to simply dance the night away, literally, as the Air Force base was having an all-night dance party that would pick up right when the Army base party ended at 2:00 a.m.

As we closed one party, we connected with a couple other friends and decided to head to the next party, but as we entered the building for the Air Force base party, we were indecisive about actually going, debating whether it was worth paying the cover charge. While we huddled around our indecision, I was approached by a nice, debonair-looking guy, all suited up, as though this was the first party of the night. His exact words were: "Would you like to dance?" I looked at him and simply stated, "I don't even know if we're going to stay yet." A little while later, still standing with my group of indecisive friends, I looked up and there he was again. He was as equally persistent as he was good looking. I must admit it was flattering that he noticed me from across the room and wanted to be the first to get a dance with me. Once I declined the dance for a second time, he kindly let me know that I should find him if I decided to stay. And I did just that. As soon as we paid the cover charge, I found him. Of course, by then he was headed to the dance floor with another young lady. This did not deter me at all. I gently tapped his shoulder, ignoring the young lady, and asked, "Do you want to dance now?" He looked at me, turned to the other woman and excused himself from dancing with her, then introduced himself as Ben and led me to the dance floor where our lives changed forever.

I always lived by three nightclub rules for myself: (1) do not to dance to the point of getting sweaty; (2) do not slow dance with anyone you are not taking home, which was no one; and (3) do not give your phone number to anyone. Well, I broke all three rules: we danced until we were both sweating, we slow danced, and I topped the night off by giving my new-found cutie-pie my phone number. My girlfriend and I left and made a bet about who would get a phone call first as she also shared her number that night.

I won the bet. Ben called me the next afternoon and from that day forward, we were inseparable. We spent every evening and weekend together, learning how we had so much more in common than just partying at the club. We discovered that we liked movies, playing pool, dining out, miniature golf, sports, and even watching the long-running soap opera *The Young and The Restless*, which we watched together each day on our lunch hours. We became an instant couple. Outside of the many "chicks" who did not want to accept that he was off the market, most accepted me as his new girlfriend. Of course, the opposition did not move me at all, as I had a lot of experience in facing opposition.

It did not take long for us to become serious, and it happened naturally. While we had a comical and eventful courtship, he was always a supporter and protector from the beginning. He had cracked the code for making me feel the level of special that my grandmother did. This was huge in that no one had ever occupied this space before, certainly not in my adult life. I was open and honest with him, and he created a space where I felt comfortable being vulnerable. This was to my benefit because within months of our dating, my biological father died and I was compelled to tell Ben the entire story of my paternity. The trauma came crashing down like it was happening in real time. My mother convinced me that it would be inappropriate for me to pay my last respects at the funeral because it would bring about too many questions as to why I was there. My brother had my mother's blessing to attend the funeral (as far as I knew) and have closure in saying his final goodbyes to our father, while I had to sit in yet another traumatic episode of my mother's negative control over my life. Ben was like my very own unlicensed therapist as he merely listened and did not judge. This opened the way for me to feel comfortable sharing bits and pieces of my life story.

I was beginning to recognize that I had been operating in a space of overcompensation. I felt the need to ensure that everything about me could not be questioned—at least not according to what I perceived as what was best. My appearance was paramount, I was an overachiever on my job, I had to get the best grades in my classes, and I had to have my apartment decorated to a certain standard. If I could take it to the next level, I did. I always felt the need to project a certain image so that it appeared everything was right in my world. I was also at a point where I felt that my newfound love had my back no matter what.

Don't get me wrong, we had the normal lover's quarrels that happen in a new relationship. Some were quite comical. Once, when my "Disco Dan" boyfriend—so called because he never missed a party—was at the nightclub, when one of his so-called friends, called my apartment and left a message on my answering machine. She mistook it to be Ben's apartment. I had his voice on my answering machine as a security measure. When I got the message, I called the female back. She confirmed that my cute, debonair boyfriend had told her that this was his place. I was so infuriated that I called the club and asked them to page him. I was going to curse him out and break up with him over the phone. The only problem was that the club told me the only way they would page him was if it was an emergency. Well, I immediately thought of one. I called the club back and told them that my apartment was on fire. When he came to the phone, I ignited a fire on him with my words and he came home to finish the argument. Needless to say, I forgave him, and we never heard from that female again.

We traveled together and discovered each other in ways that I did not deem imaginable. What was extremely impressive about my future husband was that he occupied a space of confidence—sometimes too confident—that nicely supported my larger-than-life personality. I was able to be me without playing low. He was not a "yes man"—sometimes I remind myself that I got what I asked for—and did not feel the need to be validated by anyone. It was obvious to many that he chose me. He had been in the Air Force for eight years, lived in three different countries with five different duty assignments, yet never married or had kids. I ended up in New Jersey for him to choose me.

After two years of being together, I was beginning to get anxious as I knew that this was the real husband I wanted for the rest of my life. He was not quite on the same page with me at that time. I recall Valentine's Day in 1992. Sally Jesse Raphael, Ricki Lake, and every other talk show seemed to have couples proposing on live TV. Well, I did not expect a broadcasted proposal, but I was expecting a ring and dinner. By the evening of Valentine's Day when my "Hunk of Burning Love" showed up, he had a present. It was a jogging suit and sneakers. They were nice—I had shown him what I liked—but they were not exactly a romantic Valentine's Day gift. When I got to the sneakers, I was shaking each shoe in anticipation that a ring would fall out of one of them. But no ring fell out and I was devastated. So devastated that I could not stop crying. Ben, being the empathetic man that he is, took me to dinner and explained that he planned to propose to me, but on his time. That bit of reassurance was all I needed. His own timing came later that year, Christmas of 1992. It was at 6:00 p.m. after dinner. It was all caught on tape and delivered in a heartfelt way. Little did he know that he was now going to be my official luggage handler, as I had much more baggage to unload to achieve true healing from all the trauma in my life.

We married in November of 1993. Our wedding was an emotional and memorable occasion. My mother was happy at this wedding because we had a wedding ceremony that she could boast about. I created an opportunity within the ceremony to highlight the mothers-in-law, so it painted the picture that everything was right in our worlds. It was a time when the trauma took a back seat in my mind. The wedding and reception were amazing. After all, my "til death do us part" husband and I had a lot of experience in partying as that is how we met.

We had a wonderful start to our marriage. It was the typical scenario—we started in our apartment and within a year we bought our first house. The never-ending question at the two-year mark was, "are you pregnant?" In the beginning it was fun, as we were having a lot of fun trying to conceive, but as more months passed, we began to get concerned that it was not going to happen. After a year of trying, I began to stress. I dreaded what was going to happen if I could not give my wonderful husband a child. I already knew he would be a great father. And I knew how to take care of a baby, especially with all the practice I had during my Cinderella years. The only concern was if it would become a reality for us. It didn't help any that three of my closest friends (Torrye, Kelli, and Sheila—in that order) all got pregnant when I was trying. I was happy for them, but the only thing that made it hard for me was that they all already had one child each. They were all pregnant with their second child. We were simply trying to have our first child. It was not until I woke up one morning and my husband had inscribed on the mirror, "A baby I can live without, you I cannot," that I let myself relax. I think I got pregnant that night.

We welcomed our first child, Benjamin Hunt IV—my perfect little bundle of joy. He was loved and adored by all, especially by all the kids my Fab 5 had within months of his birth—the kids are all close to this day. The love that I felt for him could not be described. Once Benjamin came along, time spent with my mother became more frequent. I cannot say that it was because of me or her new grandchild, but we were all okay with it.

My career started as an office manager and blossomed into a career in Human Resources. I had the opportunity to build HR departments in varying companies, of all sizes and industries, as well as to reengineer HR functions and processes. After the birth of my son, I began to make greater strides in my career. I was recruited out of what I thought was my dream job as a director, working only 10 minutes from my house with a weeping willow tree as the view from my office window, to land what was the most pivotal role in my career: The Vice President of Human Resources for Philadelphia Coca-Cola (now Liberty Coca-Cola).

While my career and family life were progressing and we were extremely happy, there was a new trauma that I began to deal with in the more prestigious executive role that I now occupied. It was an underlying feeling of inadequacy. The feeling had nothing to do with my overall professional, academic, leadership, or social competence. Instead, it had everything to do with the feeling that I was surrounded by people who did not have a story like mine. I felt as though I was living a lie and was ashamed that I did not come from the perfect childhood, with the loving mother-daughter relationship that so many of my colleagues could profess to have. I was further concerned that if I divulged that I did not come from what society deems to be the appropriate upbringing, I might be respected less and possibly be unable to relate at the upper echelons of corporate America. It was because of this that I remained on a constant pursuit to add tools to my professional toolbox. I was an overachiever as a mechanism of overcompensation. I did not want to look good on the outside, which was how I had gotten through my childhood, and then not be complete on the inside. I wanted to create the whole package for myself. This was my strategic approach and appeared to be working for me for the most part, but it could not help me overcome the next trauma in my life.

My baby boy, Benjamin, was about three years old when my husband and I began to try to expand our family. I desperately wanted a second son. I had a true fear of parenting a girl because of all the trauma associated with my mother and me. No matter the perspective that I reflected from, I always came to the same conclusion of not wanting to repeat the treatment I experienced, and I was so afraid that I would hurt a daughter in the same ways that I had been hurt. As I reflected on the few times when my mother wrote to me—my senior book, a few letters—or had seemed to sincerely convey that she loved me with her words, I still ended up in a place where her words did not truly align with her actions. It was because of this that I did not trust that I had it in me to give a girl child the love and attention that was not given to me.

After about nine months of trying, we found out that I had conceived and was about six weeks pregnant. We were excited, but not yet spreading the news, except to our closest friends and family.

Excited and living life to the fullest, my husband, our adorable little boy, and I were out to dinner at a local restaurant. This was not something out of the norm; however, what happened next changed my perspective on life and my family makeup forever. As we were waiting for dinner to come, we were happily watching Little Ben color on the children's handout when suddenly I felt a huge gush. I immediately excused myself and went to the ladies' room to confirm that it was blood. Thank goodness I had on tights under my black pants and it did not go through to my pants (at least not at that point). I quickly made my way back to the table to tell my husband that we needed to leave right away. He instantly headed for the car and

I got Little Ben ready to go and had the meal diverted to a "to go" meal. We got home and I called the doctor, who instructed me to go to the emergency room. At the ER, we learned the inevitable; I had just experienced a miscarriage. This came with so many mixed emotions: sadness, disappointment, guilt for being so convinced that it had to be another boy, and renewed anxiety as to whether I would be able to grow our family. At this juncture in our lives, we were spiritually grounded and could surmise that everything happened for a reason. All that said, it still did not dull the reality that I had just lost a life that had been growing inside of me.

I was forced to reevaluate my strong desire to not have a girl child. As time passed, I learned that I was in the company of other women who also had experienced miscarriages, which helped me to get through a tough time. I was given a clean bill of health to proceed in trying to have another child, and within a few months we were pregnant again. My level of happiness and relief overshadowed any concern that I had for the baby's gender. During those interim months, I had the opportunity to fully embrace that I was going to love and appreciate the child we were blessed with, regardless of the baby being a boy or girl. Not to mention that Fab 5 Sheila told me that since I was godmother to her daughter, I had to experience having a daughter. Five months into the pregnancy, I learned that I was, indeed, having a girl. I was elated for two reasons: the first being, I had grown to love Yolanda Adams' song "My Darling Girl," it became my anthem for me and my unborn daughter; and the second was, I did not have to worry about telling another little boy that he was the best little boy in the world, since that was Benjamin's title.

The anticipation continued to build as I approached the best months of pregnancy for me—the third trimester—and I was so excited for my perfect baby girl, who would be named Taylor Lynn Hunt. She was, and is, my precious baby girl. Even after having Benjamin, I did not have the revelations that came with this new baby girl. I now had the overwhelming reality of parenting from the power of choice and not just a space of love, adoration, and responsibility. I was so focused on ensuring that this baby girl could feel the love that was conveyed upon me by my grandmother that many people thought I was intoxicated with how much I doted over her. I was excited to have both a little boy and a little girl, and not slight either one of them, but rather ensure they both felt their own special place in my heart. It became and continues to be my mission to do something different in order to get a different result. I recognized that it is in my power to cause the paradigm shift in the parenting model in which my husband and I operate.

Four women have been very specific role models in mothering a girl. Deacon Felice, Sis. Lynetta, Dr. Booker, and my dear friend and confident, Brownette, all have three girls each, who they have raised successfully, have close relationships with, and have loved through all the tough years to become successful adult women. What's even more amazing about these women is how they have given me the space to come to them, always with open arms and amazing advice. They truly have shown me that it is possible to love a girl child unconditionally, and that

I do not have to repeat the cycle of mistreatment that I experienced with my daughter, my precious Taylor Lynn.

As I reframed the trauma during this time in my life, I had to face the harsh reality that I was contributing to the perpetuation of certain traumas in my life. This is what is meant by the analogy of the dirty laundry and my having to do it. I realized that I did not have to continue in a generational mode of secrecy as I had been brought up to do. I did not have to continue blaming myself for not having a close relationship with my mother. I was creating the unrealistic requirement on myself to live up to an image of a perfect childhood that no one said I had to have. I had placed pressure on myself to achieve pregnancy within a certain time frame. I had to see myself as empowered to make changes that would be critical to my life going forward. I had to determine that what had happened to me up to that point in my life was no accident, but that it equipped me with what I needed to overcome my past. I had to focus on making the change and having the courage not to be concerned with who might be offended by the changes I was making.

I invite you to take a moment to reflect on any trauma that you experienced being passed down from generation to generation. Oftentimes, hearing another person's experiences of trauma can trigger our own stories. Contemplate the things that happened when you had to create a paradigm shift and, if you are able, feel free to work openly on reframing those traumas.

The generational trauma that I have experienced that has affected my perspective is:

_____

_____

_____

_____

I make the choice to shift this paradigm in the following way:

_____

_____

_____

_____

CHAPTER NINE

FACING MY TRAUMAS AND
MY TRAUMA GIVER HEAD-ON

*Taking responsibility to effect change
for the better is within one's control,
but it is easier said than done.*

Recognizing the power of reframing, which was a key motivation for writing this book, is much easier said than done. Although I was able to reframe many of life's traumas, nothing prepared me for the trauma that would ensue when facing my trauma giver, my mother. While we had come a long way from my mother controlling me to having what I would classify as an okay relationship, there was still a significant amount of residue revealed episodically during my mother's various visits to my home. I believe we had both worked hard to show that we cared for one another, and she was building a good relationship with her grandchildren. While I was continually sharing materially, in retrospect, I realized that I was not truly sharing emotionally. This was yet another coping mechanism to not be hurt or controlled whenever she justified how she had treated me. I reached a point of wanting to deal with all the suppressed anger and hurt that I had been carrying around for so many years.

I was ultimately introduced to *The Trauma Zone*, written by R. Dandridge Collins, PhD. This book was instrumental in my healing process until I asked my mother to read the book so she could understand my perspectives and how I was feeling. I was hopeful that if she read the book it would be easier for us to discuss the various situations and circumstances that had resulted in my trauma as it related to her. It did not go as planned, but instead was like every other attempt to have a discussion with my mother about how I felt. It turned into a shouting match and her shifting things back to how she struggled to take care of my brother and me, and that her childhood was not great either. I was at a place where I realized that to heal from my trauma, I could not let it be about her and I had to stay my course in facing her as my trauma giver to get to the other side. The only problem was that she was not willing to participate. On top of everything, she looked me in my eyes and hurt me very deeply by saying, "You are my trauma." In that moment I was devastated. As a mother, I was reeling with rage. How could a mother stand in front of a child—a child who did not ask to be in this world and who is a product of her upbringing—and make all the trauma the child's fault while shifting the blame away from herself? I did not want to be disrespectful but was angry with myself for succumbing to her mean, intimidating manner by walking away without speaking my true feelings. It was as though the bandage had been ripped off and the wounds of trauma reopened. The pain was further magnified by the realization that my mother appeared to feel justified in how she treated me.

Although the trauma of rejection resurfaced, I was better equipped to deal with it at this point in my life. My husband was aware of my hope that my mother would read the book, so he was ready to help me pick up the pieces and move on despite the fact that things did not turn out as I had hoped. This still was not enough, as I was left working through some of the things that were said to me. The one that stands out most is, "God had forgiven her for what she had done." I agree 100 percent with that statement; however, as a mom I also realized the importance of taking responsibility for the collateral damage that is caused by what we do to our children. Being a mom gave me a firsthand understanding of how it all has so much to do with the power of choice. I realized that I must choose to do or not do something to my children, as there will be a consequence in their lives and mine.

"I had a tenuous and strained relationship with my father throughout my adult years. My feelings of rejection manifested in my personal and professional relationships to the point that I began pushing everyone away as a defense mechanism. At a very critical point in my career, feeling like I was 'invisible' no longer worked. I was forced to confront my own fear of rejection, which meant I had to confront my feelings. It was the only way I could experience success. I attempted to confront my father with my feelings, but he quickly dismissed me and refused to talk about it or own how his behavior impacted our family. Once again, I was devastated by his rejection. What emerged from this experience was my realization that healing is a personal journey. I could not force my father to own his behavior, but I could be responsible for my own. I forgave him for his abandonment and then forgave myself for believing the negative messages that had lived in my head for years. That moment of liberation revealed my inner strength, born from overcoming the trauma inflicted by my father. It was not easy, but it was my path to emotional freedom. I no longer felt invisible or rejected because I did the work to overcome."

—Stacy Holland, Principal of The Holland Group

Ms. Holland's experience of trauma prevented her from progressing personally and professionally. Like me, the lasting effects of trauma had both positive and negative effects on her perspective as a leader. It was not until she could overcome that trauma by dealing with the repercussions of interactions with her trauma giver that she was able to begin the healing process.

There was a direct correlation of the effects of trauma on my leadership to how I perceived the trauma. When I positioned myself in a place of empowerment instead of in a space of being victimized, whether valid or not, it allowed me to occupy the appropriate spaces that people in leadership occupy. Those spaces allow for greater transparency, vulnerability, and authenticity, all of which are leadership traits that can make the difference between good and great leadership. My capacity to operate effectively in this vein facilitated more effective leadership at all levels, from staff level to boardroom level stakeholders across varying organizations. It has been most impactful in the consultation space with CEOs.

That being said, my approach to leadership has been evolutionary in that the challenges varied from year to year and from employer to employer; however, the overarching theme remained constant. While very much in the minority, either as a woman or as a minority woman, I was always faced with having to prove that I had a comprehensive leadership style. Many of my counterparts on the same leadership teams seemed to get a pass for gaps that may have existed in their leader prowess, but that was not my story to tell. The greatest challenges were in male-dominated environments, where I felt the need to always be at the top of my game and felt I could never let them see me sweat. I was working mostly with men who were the sole providers and who had wives at home to get the kids off to school, giving the man the ability to come in early or work as late as needed. Most had gone to college and experienced the traditional college experience, unlike my story of working full time and going to school full time. We just seemed to come from very different life experiences. I could not focus on what I did not have compared to them, nor could I allow their movement to dictate mine. I had to see my experiences as a diverse perspective versus an unfortunate anomaly. I had to make the conscious decision that I needed to play the game by a set of rules that achieved results, but not at the expense of being untrue to myself and ignoring what was important to me. This is where I had an amazing example in my family—everyone had a great work ethic and I was proud of it. This included my mother, father, and grandfather, all of whom always showed their capacity to make work a priority. This was not a problem for me; the only challenge was that none of my family had reached the level of leadership in a company like I was experiencing. My work ethic coupled with all the self-esteem instilled in me by my grandmother was still not sufficient to trump the feelings of inadequacy at the C-Suite level of leadership.

A critical crossroads on my leadership journey was the Discover Leadership Training experience. Through this development opportunity I was afforded the opportunity to gain awareness of how some of my leadership characteristics could be detrimental to my long-term success. There were some extremely profound experiences that helped in my individual healing process. When Mike Jones, President/CEO Discover Leadership Training and Executive Coach, asked me the pointed question, "When will you stop achieving great things to prove someone wrong who told you that you would never be anything, instead of doing it because you want to?" This broke me down because not only did it convey that my overcompensation was obvious to others, it also made me face the fact that I was not really enjoying my success in a meaningful way. At that moment, I was set free from working to prove anything to anybody, but instead being true to achieving what made me happy and benefited my family. This was very liberating. At another point in the same program, we were in a circle of reflection and as we went around the circle, all participants shared a trauma caused by their parents. Of all the participants, which were many, only one man stopped and pondered the realization that he did not have anything negative in his life that he could attribute to his parents—he established that they were really good parents. From the time I heard that man speak, I was on a mission to be the type of parent he described—the parent whose children would not need to be healed from trauma inflicted by the parent.

I experienced many revelations and breakthroughs through my Discover Leadership experiences. The major theme of those revelations was that I was walking wounded and overcompensating in many areas of my life to ensure that everyone else was okay. It wasn't until I became equipped with the power of reframing that I was able to continue to face my traumas and to move forward in facing my trauma giver from a place of healing and not hurt.

> "When I met Tracee Hunt for the first time at the Philadelphia Coca-Cola Bottling Company, I recognized she was a strong leader. My statement to her was, 'We all occupy the largest room in the house, which is the room for improvement.' If she wanted things that she was looking at to change, she would need to change the way she was looking at them. Reframing became the foundation to create this change. Though not easy, it requires truly 'getting real' with yourself in order to have breakthrough moments."
>
> —Mike Jones, President/CEO
> Discover Leadership Training and Executive Coach

Mr. Jones witnessed Ms. Hunt firsthand as a leader who thought she had it all together, only to find out she needed to grow into the next-level leader that would catapult her into the next levels of success. Implementing all the tools I had learned in Discover Leadership was pivotal. However, I also had to do the spiritual work required to ensure that I placed my faith not in myself, but in God. At the point that I was equipped with Godly wisdom, lessons from my life of trauma, and leadership tools I was able to begin turning my trauma into tools for success. These tools transcended my marriage, my ability to create the paradigm shift in parenting, as well as in navigating my career, which paved the way for me to give back to teens like myself. Reframing was one of the key tools used to foster my own growth.

My Cinderella years prepared me for being a responsible wife. I often conveyed to my husband that my mother taught me a lot of good lessons; however, the methods in which she taught the lessons were very traumatic. I understood the importance of taking care of the house and making family a priority. I was fortunate to have a grandmother who showed me what adding affection and love to the equation was all about. It was a process for me to realize the importance of understanding that my way was not the only way. I was domesticated in an environment that was plagued with domineering opinions and little tolerance for appreciating alternative ways of doing things. I was not at all flexible in my thinking as it related to what was acceptable and not acceptable in marriage or raising kids. Thank God for a husband who is secure in himself and willing to challenge my ways of thinking. Not that his ways were all right, but his challenges created a space for compromise and for me to see things from another perspective. This was in line with the saying that I had learned in Discover Leadership: "Your map is not the territory." It took a lot of strength, humility, and courage to challenge the ideals that were so deeply ingrained in me as a child, whether good, bad, or indifferent.

It was even harder to challenge how I was going to raise my kids in ways that did not align with how I was raised. This was where my mother-induced traumas were often triggered. I recall being exhausted from the routine of parenting and having to chauffeur to and from all the sporting events and extracurricular activities, and my mother would comment, "Been there, done that." I would immediately recall the lack of support and her comment so many years ago: "I am going to one of your games since I went to one of your brother's." Did she forget that we participated in most of our sports under the direction of our grandfather? I also felt the tension when I would allow my kids to have a voice instead of silencing them with the "shut up" or "be seen and not heard" standard by which I was raised. I was not allowed to have a voice or feelings as a child. There were still times when the parenting styles that I abhorred reared their ugly heads. They would come through in behind-the-scenes conversations with my husband in comments like, "You don't get to have any opinion when you don't pay any bills." Or I could feel the anger bubbling inside of me and I really wanted to just lay into my daughter; however, I always reminded myself in an instant what it did to me, and I did not want to go down that path with my daughter.

I did not spank my kids, which was the exact opposite of my upbringing. I learned that we could create a healthy fear within our kids for doing the wrong thing without instilling an intimidating fear for our capacity of hurting them.

I can recall the profound moment when this was revealed to me. It was a time when I allowed my daughter to have her voice in the midst of getting one of my firm speeches, which I am sure included my firm and direct form of discipline. I asked her if she thought I would ever allow anyone to hurt her and she replied, "I know you won't let anyone else hurt me, but I'm not sure if you will hurt me." It crushed me to hear that she could question if I, the one who cherished the ground she walked on, could do anything to ever hurt her. I did not want to instill the same fear in her that my mother had browbeaten into me. From that moment forward, I made it my mission to ensure that even in the challenging moments I would balance the love with the lesson that had to be taught. It may not be delivered simultaneously, but there is an art to timing the follow-up message of love and support. I learned from my sweet baby girl that, as a mom, I must love my children even when they are not always easy to love, when their opinion differs from mine, when puberty is in full swing, when they are not loving on me because they want to push the envelope, and when they are mad at me because the answer is no. It takes laying down your pride and need to be right to convey a love that is contrary to the very feelings that you experience as a result of your young person's behavior. I vowed to be the parent who would put in the work to forge a bond with each of my kids that cannot be broken by life's difficult times. I continually remind myself that I birthed them and that they did not ask to be brought into this world. I want to honor them as they honor me as their parent, without provoking them in negative ways that only do damage to the parent/child relationship. I never want to be so proud or stubborn that I am not able to be vulnerable for my kids in a way that allows us to get to the best outcomes.

As I grew as a person, I adopted the following saying in my professional life: "Grow the person, grow the leader, grow the organization." It was critical in my senior HR leader role to recognize the importance of driving organizational culture through the holistic growth of the employees within the organization. I had the awareness that people cannot effectively do the amazing makeover every day when they come to work. It is virtually impossible for people to believe that they can operate one way in their personal life and then another way at work. Inevitably, things will spill over and if it is not for the good, the employee and the organization will suffer. Because of this, I became a huge proponent of ensuring that leader development efforts focus on the whole person and not just address one specific leader competence area. My growth and development from overcoming and reframing my trauma allowed me to understand the importance of placing the appropriate amount of emphasis on personal accountability as it relates to transforming organizational culture in a way that is mutually beneficial for both the employees and the organization. It is this perspective that began to shape my next-level thinking as it related to leader competence. Ultimately, it supported my capacity to deliver favorably in the space of executive consultation in a wide array of industries in companies of varying sizes.

It was never enough for me to just operate effectively in the workplace. It was equally important for me to effectuate change and give back to young inner-city youth who might have stories like mine. I always stated that I have a heart for young people. Early in my tenure as VP of HR at Coca-Cola, I got involved in youth initiatives with Philadelphia's youth system. I had the fortunate opportunity to chair the Philadelphia Youth Council, which included the launch of Project U-Turn, an initiative that was designed to reconnect out-of-school youth back to education to achieve their high school GED. The culminating events for the summer youth program were amazingly rewarding, as I could identify with inner city youths' desires to achieve in spite of their circumstances. Having the opportunity to be an example of succeeding at various levels, overcoming obstacles, and then giving back has been amazing and therapeutic. This work continues to be fulfilling for me. I know the work that I support through meaningful board participation ultimately impacts the lives of young people.

"Having a board member like Tracee Hunt has been invaluable to my organization's impact and to my personal growth as a leader. In order to influence and nurture youth, leaders need to share their experiences—positive and negative—and be an example of overcoming. It is only through this that there can be a connection. But it is not easy to get to that place. When community leaders like Tracee share of themselves, they are a motivation to others. Transforming trauma into triumph is possible when we are able to reflect, grow, and apply what we have learned to help others. Tracee has done all three and the evidence is in the lives that she has impacted through her service."

—Chekemma Fulmore Townsend,
CEO of the Philadelphia Youth Network

Ms. Townsend made it her mission to give young people the opportunity to become successful individuals, no matter what kind of traumas they have experienced. Executives who have overcome their own traumas act as youth mentors in the Philadelphia Youth Network (PYN). As a board member of PYN, giving back to the community has been part of my healing process. Reframing during this time was a process that required me to tap into my capacity to encourage myself and to move forward on many different fronts. I had too much riding on what I stood to gain instead of what I stood to lose by not coming out on the other side—the other side being one of healing and wholeness. The alternative would have resulted in marginal achievement, as I would have been in a vicious cycle of achieving for the wrong reasons. I had to make the conscious choice to channel all my tools toward maximizing my successes in every aspect of my life—marriage, parenting, career, and giving back.

I invite you to take a moment to reflect on the possibility of facing the person(s) who caused you trauma. Oftentimes, hearing another person's experiences of trauma can trigger our own stories. Contemplate the pros, cons, and possibility that you may not get the response you desire and, if you are able, feel free to work openly on reframing those traumas.

The person(s) who have caused my trauma are:

_____

_____

_____

_____

_____

_____

The pros and cons of facing my trauma giver are:

_____

_____

_____

_____

_____

_____

Tools that I can use to support my healing process are:

_____

_____

_____

_____

_____

_____

CHAPTER TEN

STANDING UNAPOLOGETICALLY IN MY TRUTH AND BEING AN UNCOMPROMISING LEADER

There is liberty in transparency.

It became more comfortable for me to tell my truth once I no longer had the desire to portray the image that I had an upbringing that others had to approve. I began to open-up routinely about bits and pieces of my upbringing, mistakes, and life choices. I found that all these things were the ingredients fueling me as a multidimensional leader. The leader with a highly effective emotional quotient (EQ) coupled with leader competence and instinct, was a combination for driving cultural transformation and serving as a strong, uncompromising leader. For years I glossed over where I came from—at least the real details—for fear that I would be perceived as less than. Once I came to the realization that my story was one of courage and not defeat, I began to draw the correlations of how my life's traumas were the steppingstones to my success. Coming from the inner city without a "silver spoon" equipped me to relate to employees at all levels, though I occupied a seat in the C-Suite. I operated with a level of humility and transparency that allowed me to connect with the most challenging leaders at all levels. In the same vein, the level of empathy that I possessed allowed me to meet people where they were, no matter their path in life. This proved to be very beneficial for me as it related to gaining trust across all stakeholders.

I operated with a fortitude and endurance that was second to none, given that I had put myself through college with little to no financial support from family. Work ethic was something that came natural for me as I did have many examples of how hard work pays off, especially from my mother—I give credit where credit is due. It was interesting to me how people would ask what my parents did for a living. This is an area where I could proudly say that I had some really great role models in the world of work. I am a living example in this regard as it relates to the saying, "Kids don't do what you say, they do what they see."

Being an executive in a male-dominated workforce did not come without challenges. I had to occupy the space of collaborative leader, forceful advocate, and strategic advisor as well as to acquiesce among leaders, all in a day's work, without compromising who I was or what I stood for as a woman, wife, and mother. I always operated with a level of poise and determination to be successful in an environment that called for a multidimensional leader. I was successful walking the production or warehouse floor, and equally as effective in the boardroom. There was always the delicate balance of being a trusted leader to both the employees and management alike. I learned that the art to this balance was to operate in integrity and to be true to myself in the highs and the lows.

I felt accomplished in that I successfully transformed a critical organizational function, effectively managed annual HR budgets in excess of seven figures, and effectuated sustainable change for the organization through various stages of the business lifecycle. I continue to serve on various boards of directors, leading committees and serving in appointed positions, supporting many meaningful causes, and helping a myriad of constituencies.

In addition to many amazing accomplishments, I had the opportunity to meet many distinguished individuals during my C-Suite years. The two occasions that stand out most are when I met President Bill Clinton—of whom I took the worst picture of my life because I was overexcited—and when I met Prince Charles and the Duchess of Cornwall. Both Prince Charles and the President were extremely personable and made each person they encountered feel as though they had their undivided attention—they truly have the gift of charisma.

At this juncture, I was experiencing a steady stream of success. I had the day-to-day challenges that every working mother is faced with (the balancing act), but I was growing spiritually, emotionally, and professionally.

Just as I was getting comfortable in my skin and in my groove as an executive, life happened. My role as an executive for one of the most well-known brands in the world was coming to an end as a large-scale reorganization was on the horizon. What initially appeared to be an unfortunate situation provided another opportunity to be part of a transition team that offered me valuable experience. I could now add large-scale work stream management to my repertoire of weighty transformational experiences, which already included building HR, transforming HR, leading HR through mergers and acquisitions, culture transformation, and organization restructuring. This was the opportunity to see the glass as half full, a time when the saying, "Change is inevitable, but growth is optional," came to life. I was not going to allow this time in my life to take on the attributes of trauma that had plagued me in so many ways throughout my life. I was determined to turn this monumental change into something great.

"I admire Tracee so much. She is an incredible leader—a person who, when you look back on your career, stood out and made an impact on the organization and your life. We literally had to create a credible human resource function in a longstanding organization that could be characterized as nonexistent. Her intrinsic leadership style diffused many tough situations within a male-dominated organization and a tough teamster environment. She was strong, resolute, and determined, while also expressing incredible caring for associates. She cared about people and it was genuine. Her journey to get to that stage had not been an easy one. To become a leader, she had to learn to overcome her own perceived weaknesses, communicate effectively, and disperse of any prejudices."

—Fran McGorry, Owner and CEO of Liberty Coca-Cola
(formerly Philadelphia Coca-Cola)

Mr. McGorry saw my fortitude as a young female executive navigating a male-dominated world, balancing the needs of the employees and the needs of the organization, while sustaining my integrity without compromising myself as a woman and a leader. I was finally beginning to see myself as an overcomer. I was at a stage in my life where I did not have to reframe what was happening, but I was able to reflect on how all my experiences shaped the person I had become.

I invite you to take the opportunity to reflect on how your trials and traumas have shaped you in a positive way into the person that you are. You may not feel that you have arrived; however, give yourself credit for any progress you have made.

Begin to see your trials as building blocks for your character. See your trauma as motivation to effectuate change in your life and those around you for the better.

Trials I have faced in my life that I can use as building blocks are or have been:

_____

_____

_____

_____

Trauma that I have experienced has motivated me in the following ways:

_____

_____

_____

_____

CHAPTER ELEVEN

TRAUMA FREE—LIVING LIFE FROM A PLACE OF HEALING AND WHOLENESS

*The journey of healing and wholeness
is perpetual, and ever so rewarding.*

By no means do I feel that I have arrived. I am constantly learning and growing along my journey. The healing process is perpetual and must remain a conscious choice. This is because there are always situations and triggers that can challenge the space of healing and wholeness. My transition from employee to entrepreneur has been a true testament to my healing, and reframing has paved the way to a life where challenges are readily overcome. More importantly, every challenge is now seen as a lesson instead of a trauma, which was the lens I operated from in the past.

I often say that I made it my mission to major in accounting, vocational education, and human resources so that I would always have a job and never have to return home. Little did I know that the combination of education and focusing on my HR goals would be complimentary in the business world, but also prove to be beneficial in so many ways beyond just remaining gainfully employed. My astute business acumen, by way of accounting knowledge, served me well in the boardroom as I could hold my own with key executives in varying organizations. My degree in vocational education with an emphasis in HR training and development afforded me the fundamentals in writing competency-based training programs that have proven useful throughout my career in HR as it relates to learning and development. My HR education and career experience has opened doors that are tailor-made for my compilation of knowledge, skills, and abilities, allowing me to hold key roles in varying industries and organizations of various sizes. I often describe it as being in the right place at the right time—a lot of times. Ultimately, this resulted in me now operating my company, Total HR Solutions, LLC, with a competitive edge that sets it apart from other HR consulting firms.

There was no direct path to get here and, though fully worthwhile, it has not been an easy journey. Transitioning to the world of entrepreneurship from the corporate world was a monumental blow to my self-image that had to be redefined. I knew I wanted to start my own company; however, I did not want to be thrust into it based on the reorganization timing of Coca-Cola. So, to my good fortune, within a couple months of transitioning out of a company with the most well-known brand in the world, I then accepted a key executive role in a regionally known not-for-profit. This opportunity further prepared me for the not-for-profit clients I would service in my business. I accepted the opportunity, but, made it clear that it was temporary as I was going to be starting my own business in two years, and I did just that. Though I was making the moves that would inevitably move me closer to my goals, there were some side effects I had not considered. While I had established a solid footprint in my region, I was not prepared for the internal perception that I cast on myself. For the 15 years prior, I had been able to identify with a weighty title affiliated with a well-known entity. I was now the founder and CEO of a company of two: me and my assistant. It was probably a dose of the law of reciprocity. When I was a high-level executive, I would unconsciously minimize leaders of small companies, not taking into account all the hard work that goes into small businesses. I realized that I was truly misinformed. This was a revelation that my self-image does not have to be attached to a title or an organization, but that it resides within how I see myself separate and apart from anything or anyone.

The revelations did not stop there, as the levels of awareness grew me as a person and as a leader. I have been charged with growing my team and it has been my mission to ensure that I am the example of diversity, equity, and inclusion. This is an area that has come easily to me because I always operated from a place of "everyone is differently important." However, when I began to grow my team and take on new client accounts, I had the most profound awareness—an awareness that did not even occur when I completed my capstone project upon graduating from the Diversity Leadership Academy at Penn State Great Valley. That awareness was regarding the LGBTQ community. In the same way that racism is learned, homophobia is a learned perspective and behavior. It takes great courage to forgo judging others and instead offer them love and respect. As individuals, we must own our actions and the lifestyles we choose. It was my strong admiration for one of my diligent colleagues that allowed me to experience this paradigm shift in my own thinking because, until then, my perspectives to never mistreat anyone were a result of my upbringing and learned beliefs and not from the additional awareness gained.

I have learned much in this chapter of my life as a business owner, mother of grown children, and wife of 27 years. There is true liberty in transparency. Operating unapologetically in my truth without concern for what people will say is who God has called me to be.

I have reached a point where I clearly recognize that each and every trauma in my life positioned me for the joys and challenges of entrepreneurship and creating the legacy I will leave for my children. I learned that it is my dash that is important—what happens from birth until my last day. I know for certain from experience that it is not where I started, but where I will finish. In this moment, though the journey is in full swing, it is not about reframing, but about celebrating.

Take this opportunity to look at where you are at this point in your life. Whether it is where you want to be or not, encourage yourself to find something that you can celebrate that will motivate you to reach for the next win that you can celebrate later. The celebration can be whatever makes you feel good, provided it is not harmful to your well-being. Do not allow anything or anyone to talk you out of reframing to get there, if needed. Use whatever tools and resources you need to get to a place of celebration for your own sake. This was key in supporting my healing and journey toward wholeness.

I choose to celebrate the following:

_____

_____

_____

_____

The reframe needed to do so is:

_____

_____

_____

_____

I am going to celebrate in the following way:

_____

_____

_____

_____

CHAPTER TWELVE

WHAT'S REALLY BEHIND THE SMILE

Never judge a book by its cover.

The smile may not be that of a baby born of rejection and pain, but of a baby who fought for survival. The smile may not be that of a little girl who did not have the love of her parents, but of a little girl whose grandmother loved her with a fierceness beyond measure. The smile may not be that of a child who grew up in a dogmatic environment, but of a child who overcame the control to be open-minded to the world around her. The smile may not be that of a student who was the product of an inner-city public school system, but of a student who flourished in academia as she earned her Masters' degree. The smile may not be that of a young lady who left home and never returned, but that of a young lady who found her independence through sheer grit and determination. The smile may not be that of mother who was never given a blueprint for maternal love from her own biological mother, but that of a mother who learned that maternal instincts could be experienced and learned from the women around her. The smile may not be that of a businesswoman who had to overcome her own insecurities in the corporate world, but that of a successful businesswoman who broke barriers to find her own voice and uplift others as well.

Best of all, believe that this smile is one of authenticity, as it deliberately conveys the desire to spread joy and warmth among all. This smile is that of a sister who treasures her brothers. This smile is that of a wife who is forever grateful to the soul connection she has in her husband. This smile is that of a mother who thanks God daily for the blessings that are her two children. This smile is that of a woman who is healed and whole and has found forgiveness for her own mother. It is the smile of a Silent Overcomer.

Key life lessons that I have learned and continue to live by:

1. Each trial is designed uniquely for me because each is a steppingstone for my own character building.
2. Never minimize any person along your journey because they all have a purpose.
3. The growth and investment of the inner being is as essential as anything that can be done for the outer being.
4. Looks are not as deceiving as one might think.

5. The more flexible and agile you are, the faster you can move beyond the sting of failure and disappointment. Change is inevitable, growth is optional.

6. When we do not place attachment to an outcome, it leaves us open to the greatest possibilities.

7. Collaboration will generate a greater outcome than going it alone.

8. Don't allow what you give and do for others to be hindered by their response or lack thereof.

9. Everything in life is about choice and you are the one with the power to choose.

10. The journey to new possibilities and creating paradigm shifts can be lonely; however, the people who are supposed to be there will be.

11. If and when you have children, recognize that just because you are the parent, you are not always right.

12. Never underestimate the power of authenticity and love.

My hope is that reading this book encourages and inspires you to create the change that is needed by reframing any and every situation that has caused trauma in your life. It's not about achieving any particular level of success, but creating a space for healing and wholeness that can facilitate individual well-being. I personally encourage you to stay the course toward becoming a Silent Overcomer.

AFTERWORD

Mike Jones

*S*ilent Overcomer is a prescription for healing from which most people will benefit. It does not matter who you are; we all have life experiences that can be regarded as traumatic. Quite often, these events are circumstances that are beyond our control.

Through the chapters you've just completed, Tracee Hunt offers each of us an incredible gift. By telling us the story of the traumatic events of her life, she gives us the realization that no matter what we have been through, we can reframe events from a negative to a positive. It is important to be aware that Tracee is in no way suggesting that you should "get over" the traumatic events that have occurred in your life; however, she is clearly communicating that there comes a time when you need to get on with living your life. To live life to its fullest, we must release ourselves from the traumas that prevent us from reaching our true potential.

Tracee made the choice to reframe the negative events that occurred in the relationship she experienced with her mother and the positive lessons she learned during what she referred to as her "Cinderella years," which allowed her to create a path to become an amazing wife for Ben and an incredible mother for Ben IV and Taylor. As we observed Tracee's journey from childhood through young adulthood and the relationships she had with her mother and grandmother, we became aware that everything occurring to her in those relationships had a frame around them. It was clear to us as she described her journey that the positive framed events picked her up and made her feel worthy, while the negative framed events made her feel unwanted and undeserving. Reframing events she experienced allowed Tracee to change her perspective, forgive her mother, and realize she was worthy of the successes she was creating.

Tracee clearly articulated how difficult it was to be a Silent Overcomer from her childhood trauma, and she provided you with an opportunity at the conclusion of each chapter to wipe the smoke off your personal mirror and identify your own trauma. Once you identified the trauma, she provided you with an opportunity to transform some of the negative events of your life into positive, new realities moving forward.

Silent Overcomer is an amazingly vulnerable look at Tracee's life, what healed her, and her insights that have the potential of healing others.